CHILDREN AS INDIVIDUALS

CHILDREN AS INDIVIDUALS

MICHAEL FORDHAM

FREE ASSOCIATION BOOKS / LONDON

Published in 1994 by
Free Association Books Ltd
Omnibus Business Centre
39–41 North Road
London N7 9DP

A CIP record for this book is available from
the British Library.

ISBN 1 85343 385 3

99 98 97 96 95 94

6 5 4 3 2 1

Designed, typeset and produced for Free Association Books
by Chase Production Services, Chipping Norton, OX7 5QR.
Printed and bound by CPI Group (UK) Ltd, Croydon, CR0 4YY

Contents

PREFACE

For this third edition of *Children as Individuals* the framework has been retained and my central thesis about the importance of the self in childhood remains the same.

Over the years, however, there has accumulated a great increase in our knowledge of intra-uterine life and of infancy. That knowledge has come from methods of observation and experimental studies operating hand in hand. It has greatly strengthened the view of an infant as an individual and has made it possible to clarify and expand the postulates on which I have worked.

This volume was originally published, with a different title, *The Life of Childhood*, with the object of introducing a theory and practice of child psychotherapy which was characteristically Jungian. Before the time it was written there was virtually no interest in child psychology amongst Jungian analysts, and consequently there were no Jungians, except myself, practising child psychotherapy in any part of the world.

The situation today is different, and there is a quite rapidly growing interest in child therapy amongst Jungian analysts with the development of a number of training centres in different parts of the world. But there is mostly interest in play therapy as instigated by Dora Kalff in Zurich. That is, I think, largely due to the 'sand tray' method, instigated by Margaret Lowenfeld, which shows that children depict archetypal themes in their play, thus confirming my own view, because the exercise is therapeutic. There was nothing novel about that, for play as therapy had been widely practised in varying contexts. A graphic illustration which impressed me had been given by Margaret Gardner in her book *The Children's Play Centre* (1937).

I had, however, gained the conviction that something deeper and more analytic could be developed with children and the present volume gives the process by which I developed that view. That accounts for the structure of the volume. First there is a chapter on 'Antecedents', which gives the assumptions, right or wrong, with which I started to work with children in distress. The next chapter records excerpts of my findings, having in mind the idea, which I soon found to be erroneous, that archetypal experiences are dangerous for children.

The material in which these forms had been studied in adults was predominently dreams and pictures, such as are found in active imagination. It was therefore these that I investigated with particular interest, adding play, which is such a prominent feature of childhood and which started Jung off on his 'confrontation with the unconscious'.

It is from all this material that theoretical formulations began to emerge, so it is logical to follow the chapters on 'Play', 'Dreams' and 'Pictures' with the theoretical structures that I formulated and which made a framework for the deeper analytic excursions on which I was embarking. I am impressed by the correctness of that procedure, which evades too much use of clinical material as illustrating some abstract formulation, though I did not fail to speculate. It is, however, upon experience that our whole theoretical structures ultimately depend; and not on the exercise of reason, as some philosophers and thinkers would have us believe.

There is much which is not included in this volume: it does not include the good work on family groups, or other studies of groups as a therapeutic exercise. But this volume is a study of children as individuals, though that must inevitably include their participation in groups. But, following Jung, I held and still do hold that therapy in its deeper sense is an individual matter and it is with that I am primarily concerned.

ACKNOWLEDGEMENTS

I wish to acknowledge with gratitude the generosity of the late William Moody of the London Child Guidance Clinic, as it was then called, for his support and encouragement in early years; the late A.E. Newth of the Nottingham Child Guidance Clinic, and R.D. Newton, director of the child guidance clinic at the Paddington Clinic and Day Hospital, for permission to publish case studies; the Society of Analytical Psychology for agreeing to let me include material published in the *Journal of Analytical Psychology*; Dr Gerd Biermann for agreeing to my publishing the case of Billy, also recorded in the *Handbuch für Kinderpsychotherapie*, edited by Dr Biermann. Professor and Mrs Jung and Mrs James Kirsch all gave criticism and valuable support in times of uncertainty when I was not sure whether what I was doing was either Jungian or analytic. But it was my late wife who listened, discussed and made suggestions in detail to every part of the original edition.

In making my revisions for the third edition I am greatly indebted to James Astor, who has worked over my alterations and made many helpful suggestions.

1 ANTECEDENTS

Throughout his life, Jung relied on the broad distinction between conscious and unconscious structures. In his enumeration of them he defined a single entity, the ego, to represent the centre of consciousness. The more obscure and complex elements in the unconscious proved numerous. They fascinated him and he devoted the main bulk of his scientific life to the study of them. He began by distinguishing two levels: the personal and collective. The first was composed of experiences which have been repressed because they are incompatible with moral or social attitudes: they are essentially parts of the ego and so can become conscious again if the barrier of repression is removed. The contents of the second differ from the first in being essentially unconscious; they can only become partly conscious through the imagery of dream and fantasy, which develop as maturation proceeds: by studying these he developed a theory of the 'collective unconscious' which sought to explain the generality of themes that he demonstrated. He also employed an amplifying phrase, the 'objective psyche', to underline a characteristic of their nature and his view that the 'inner world' of man, which they represent, is just as much an object of study as the outer world of material things and people.

As Jung's study proceeded he discovered that the data originating in the collective unconscious could be grouped together and classified, and he inferred that there were a number of centres or nodal points which expressed themselves over and over again in similar ways and displayed similar aims and functions. These centres were called archetypes of the collective unconscious, which is therefore a term used to cover the sum total of archetypes. The archetypes have been described by him as the shadow, the animus and the anima, the wise old man, the child, etc. All of them were conceived as 'non-ego' and were essentially incapable of becoming completely conscious.

A terminological problem frequently arises here from the tendency to confuse the unconscious archetype with its representation in consciousness, i.e. its imagery. There are different positions which have been taken up on this subject but in this book I shall treat the archetype as a theoretical entity said to be unconscious and refer to the images that can be grouped by using the theory of archetypes as 'archetypal', i.e. they have the characteristics which the theory requires of them: thus the mother archetype is postulated as giving rise, when brought into relation with a real mother, to images of her which contain archetypal characteristics. In short the image is defined by using a relevant adjective to distinguish it from the archetype itself.

The theory has been criticised because it was supposed to imply the inheritance of ideas and images, and it is true that in the literature formulations are presented which are vulnerable to this attack. Jung himself, in reply, reformulated his ideas so as to define the archetype as the substrate which used, as it were, sensory experience in predetermined ways to produce typical imagery. It is from my position a pity that he never drove home the conclusions in publications about childhood. His earlier ideas in this field are the latest in so far as they refer to maturation in childhood and the nature of unconscious processes in that period in the life of the individual.

THE METHOD OF ANALYTICAL PSYCHOLOGY

Having defined his field of study Jung set out to describe in detail the behaviour of archetypal images. To do so he employed four techniques which aimed to raise the contents of the collective unconscious to consciousness: free, but more often controlled association, dream analysis, active imagination, and amplification. Of these the first is well understood, the second will be treated of at more length in Chapter 7. Only the last two need introduction here, especially since they are characteristic of Jung's approach.

At some time in treatment a patient may become aware of processes which he can only dimly perceive and which he finds it difficult to express in ordinary language. When this occurs, Jung supported tendencies in the patient to let his imagination work on its own with minimal interference from the ego. If the correct time has been chosen there follows an organised fantasy taking the form of a dream in which the patient then learns how to participate as one of the figures; in this way a dialectic can develop between the ego and the archetypal imagery called active imagination. The process is facilitated by dancing, painting, carving wood or modelling clay.

It was in the material produced during active imagination that Jung unearthed, in individuals, data corresponding closely to themes of myths, rituals, magical and religious practices. Here was a mine of information throwing light on the fantasies of his patients and he accordingly started to compare the two.

Sometimes it seems as if the comparative method called amplification which he developed is a sort of intellectual *tour de force*, and so it can be; but this is not how Jung meant it to be used. He rather intended it as a development of the natural process he found taking place in his patients.

Study of a series of dreams or fantasies shows that the themes interlace and shed light on, that is amplify, each other till they lead to a central core of meaning. A good example is to be found in the dream series published in *Psychology and Alchemy* (C.W.12)*. The intellectual amplification, based on the theory of archetypes, is contained in the second part of his book, though he also gave shorter parallels to the dreams themselves.

During analytical therapy the assembly of parallels has always been considered secondary (in my view it is not necessary) to the analytic procedure itself. However, knowledge of symbolic material has been greatly increased by the comparative study of myths and the conclusions arrived at are used by analysts in their interpretation of patients' material.

What then is the value of the intellectual method of amplification? It is a teaching and research method and by using it in these ways Jung formulated a number of challenging theories about the evolutionary processes in civilisation. Foremost amongst them was his thesis that alchemy was not only a compensatory development to the Christian religion but also the precursor of the psychology of the unconscious as well as of chemistry.

---

* *Collected Works*, vol. 12. References to this edition of Jung's work are shown by using the abbreviation C.W. followed by the volume number.

CHILDHOOD

It is necessary to turn to Jung's early work, when he was influenced by Freud and whilst he was breaking away from him, to find much about the psychology of childhood. There is indeed a considerable literature here which has been largely overlooked. The most weighty publications were his studies with association tests which showed for the first time the far-reaching effects of identifications between parents and children, and how a child's life might be, so it seemed, almost completely determined by the nature of his parents. But alongside them, summarised in his lectures delivered at Clark University (1916a), he also described the sexual investigations of a little girl, Anna, (published in C.W.17). It was a companion piece to 'Little Hans', published by Freud, but Jung gave far more attention to symbolic investigations forming the basis for developing cognitive thought processes; greater respect was also given to her inner world.

His book *The Theory of Psychoanalysis* (published in C.W.4), summarises his differences from Freud but also contains much of interest for the study of child development even today, but he was being so heavily attacked by psychoanalysts at that time (1913) that its value became obscured. In it are views, then new, which are now, if not established, at least no longer made the subject of such energetic polemic (c.f. Abraham 1914). His emphasis on the importance of separating infantile sexuality from its adult form and the nutritional from the sexual instinct need no longer cause much disturbance, especially since the enormous emphasis given to hunger, greed and aggression in conjunction with sexuality in the infant's life, particularly by Klein. His assertion that the oedipal situation is a myth – not in the sense that it is unreal, but rather that it is archetypal in nature, and so is inherent in healthy child development – was first repudiated, only eventually to be accepted by psychoanalysts.

It is well worth remembering, too, that in the psychology of the unconscious he stressed the inevitability of the dual mother fantasy so important in Klein's work and traced the oedipal conflicts into the two-body mother–child relationship which lay behind and before the three-body situations to which Freud had given central importance. In this volume he also developed a far-reaching but much neglected theory about the importance of rhythm in the transformation of primitive instinctual drives into cultural activities.

It cannot be this part of his early work, which he never repudiated, that led him away from child analysis, nor, I think, was it his experimental demonstration of identification processes (C.W.4); it was rather the conclusion that if so much that was previously thought to be environmental was really innate, if the dual mother theme and the oedipal conflict were part of healthy growth, why go unearthing them? Is it not the ongoing 'tasks of life' which the child has before him which merit more attention? Better, he thought, to provide a good environment for the child and avoid stimulating regressive processes in him. Pushed to its extreme this ongoing theory, though useful, does not hold when applied to child psychopathology because it is not only parents who contribute to it.

His later lectures on education (C.W.17), though not excluding analysis of children, restrict the scope of their psychopathology and lay far greater emphasis on the influence of parents. There is scarcely anything new about the psychology of children in his later published work, though he made an interesting contribution on gifted children (in C.W.17). Yet the importance of fixation in the development of neuroses and psychoses cannot really be brushed aside: Jung did not completely ignore it, but his ongoing theory was inspired by his work on human individuation in adult persons and this distracted his attention away from child analysis.

Taking Jung's work as a whole, however, there is small justification for the idea that psychopathology is *only* the result of a child's introjecting or identifying with the less desirable unconscious processes in his parents. At the same time, when first developed – and Jung was not the only one to take this position – the thesis about the often decisive importance of parents was relevant and needed. After justifiably suffering partial eclipse because it mistakenly became a dogma that denies individuality to children, it has lately been revived: the importance of parent pathology in interfering with, perverting or obstructing ongoing maturational processes in their children has gained increasing and more balanced recognition.

In my opinion Jung, without crystallising his views on these problems, certainly felt that childhood was not worth investigating till his more important work on later life had received adequate development and recognition. Yet it was always evident that unless his concept of archetypes could be applied to childhood his theory was vulnerable to damaging criticism. Therefore it could be no surprise that in later years he started to meet the challenge, which the first edition of this book also attempted, by applying the technique of amplification to children's dreams. His results were collected in a number of seminar reports, but his views never reached formal publication.

Amongst the early pioneering analysts, Frances Wickes alone did much work with children. Her book, *The Inner World of Childhood* (1966), is a sympathetic and illuminating amplification of what Jung has suggested. To her must be given the credit of making the first application of the type theory to childhood and devising some ingenious methods of managing their primitive affective processes. Perhaps more important even was her success in popularising the idea that it was through unconscious identifications that parental influence led to many abnormalities in child development. The conclusion that if parents wish to provide a good environment for their children they should look after their own mental health, though needed when it was written, today seems rather banal, but Wickes, following Jung, gave significant impetus to refining a concept that only too easily plays on common prejudice.

In her work Wickes objects to investigating unconscious processes in children, and this thesis still influences many analytical psychologists who overlook that, in spite of her desire not to apply theories to childhood, she was dominated by no longer valid theoretical beliefs about Jung's speculative views about the nature of the inherited structures in children, such as the following: 'In ['the infantile germinal state'] are hidden not merely the beginnings of adult life, but also the whole ancestral heritage, which is of unlimited extent' (C.W.8, p.51).

Fascinating as such ideas may be, and it should be made clear that Jung later modified them, evidence for them is scanty, and what there is can be subjected to other, more credible, interpretation. However, Wickes' intuitive gifts were of a very high order, and so she records data of permanent interest, spoilt, however, by insufficient attention to detail. Her very gifts make her omit data, seemingly so small, which are essential if her observations are to be correctly evaluated in the light of present knowledge. Her repeated reference to 'the child', in particular, has become too general to be of much use; also the ages of the children to which she refers are, though very much needed, often omitted altogether, and the relevant parts of their histories are not made available.

THE AIM OF DEVELOPMENT

An essential element in Jung's theme was the importance of development. Thus he emphasises that the aim of a child's development is to reach maturity. To do this he needs to strengthen his ego so that he may exercise control over his inner and outer environment: he must also accept collective standards, almost, it sometimes seems, whatever the consequences to himself. It is in reality open to question whether this results in a true development at all and, as I shall be considering the maturation of the child in a different light and shall relate it to individuating processes using conceptions derived from Jung, it may be necessary to consider shortly how he conceived the relation of individuation to collective adaptation.

Jung (1923) contrasted the collective aims with individuation as follows:

> In general, [individuation] is the process of forming and specialising the individual nature; in particular it is the development of the psychological individual as differentiated from the general collective psychology . . . Before individuation can be taken for a goal, the educational aim of adaptation to the necessary minimum of collective standards must first be attained. (pp.661–2)

According to the main trend of Jung's work, and within the context of his analytic studies, individuation is mostly conceived to begin in persons approaching middle age; then the projections of the collective psyche into the world have to be withdrawn so that they may be considered in relation to the individual and not just accepted because they are 'what everybody does, thinks and feels'. A child, on the contrary, he maintains, must leave a large part of his psyche projected into the world and adapt himself 'to the necessary minimum of collective standards' within which he can develop his personal life. This, it would follow, is all the more important to him since he does not need to give deep consideration to what is generally accepted and the social, political and religious views of the day cannot be influenced by children. But, as children mature, they hold heterodox views about these subjects, usually as part of their rebellion against current viewpoints, on which they express themselves with considerable certainty. Thus they tend to take a one-sided or collective view as contrasted with an individual position.

According to Jung individuation also involves becoming free from opposites through an irrational or symbolical solution; to do this the opposites must be given complete equality.

> When the opposites are given complete equality of right, attested to by the ego's unconditioned participation in both thesis and antithesis, *a suspension of the will results*; for the will can no longer be operative while every motive has an equally strong counter motive by its side. Since life cannot tolerate suspension, a damming up of vital energy results, which would lead to an insupportable condition from the tension of the opposites did not a new reconciling function arise which could lead above and beyond the opposites. (1923, p.607)

Thus, individuation is conceived to involve a goal opposite to that of childhood, when strengthening the ego is all important; the goal of individuation appears, on the contrary, only when 'a suspension of the will results'.

To individuate, this theory contends, it is necessary first to relate to the archetypes, which contain the possibility of a symbolical solution to the clash of opposites but, though the process is much the same as in childhood, the aim is conceived to be entirely different. Thus relationship to the archetypes is only made when individuation is the conscious goal, decided upon by an adult man or woman, whilst a child simply cannot help being in touch with archetypal forms and processes.

The problems of children, which are closely related to ego maturation and in Jung's view can lead to ego dominance, were also seen in terms of psychological types. Jung distinguished two attitude-types, the extraverted and the introverted, and four function-types; two rational – thinking and feeling; two irrational – sensation and intuition. Any particular individual belongs to a type when he habitually adapts best with one attitude and function. This does not mean that the other attitudes and functions are absent all the time; they are simply inferior, latent, or repressed – it is often not clear which. The problem of a child was conceived as establishing his best attitude and function. In this way he gets support for his inferior status and can progressively feel himself to be more and more efficient and supposedly self-reliant. A young man can then delegate, by means of projection, the other functions to other people; when he falls in love, for instance, the woman generally holds the projection of his inferior side or anima and there results a psychologically as well as a biologically useful relationship. The reason why a child has to develop and rely upon his superior function is that the inferior one contradicts the superior: introversion contradicts extraversion, thinking contradicts feeling, and intuition contradicts sensation; if he accepts all he will be thrown back into the problem of the opposites, between which he is supposed to swing and from which he needs to free himself. This is the basis for children finding ideal figures such as the hero who fights against his opposite.

I have rendered the contrast between individuation and ego growth rather starkly because it was this opposition which dominated the scene when I wrote the first edition of this book. The grandeur and scope, the religious element and the social importance of individuation were in the centre of interest.

The definition of individuation in *Psychological Types* leaves room, however, for a different view. 'Individuation,' Jung says, 'is practically the same as the development of consciousness out of the original *state of identity*' (1923, p.563), and elsewhere, as Jacobi details, he leaves room for the idea of individuation being a continuing process throughout the whole span of a lifetime. This opening has been filled in by a number of analytical psychologists but it never received detailed attention and development till Jacobi did so in her book *The Way of Individuation* (1967). To her therefore must be given the credit of being the first to work out this line of thought.

It is therefore with regret that I cannot accept either her own or other less complete formulations. They all rely either on concepts such as that individuation is an 'instinct', or they imply a long-ranging teleology which has long been dispensed with in biology, and in my opinion with good reason. Further Jacobi in particular holds, if I understand her rightly, that the biological and adaptational aims of youth and the development of the ego are part of, but only preliminaries to, a development necessary for the processes, usually called individuation, to mature in the second half of life.

That conception has this difficulty: increase in adaptation to social requirements cannot be part of individuation if detachment from social requirements is a central feature of individuation. I am not averse to paradox or contradiction where it covers symbolic data which cannot be abstracted without loss. However, individuation is in my view a central concept related to definable processes and is not a symbol, so the paradox is not justifiable nor, I think, is it necessary. In the present book I shall demonstrate, I hope conclusively, that individuating processes are active in infancy and childhood, and that they are an essential feature of maturation.

In setting out to show this I shall make use of Jung's conceptions, though his formulations are not consistent (c.f. Fordham 1985b). On the one hand he defined the self as the totality of the psyche, comprising the ego and the archetypes, a conception which means that these structures are the parts of the whole. On the other hand he thought of the self as an entity which organises all the parts and is superordinate or transcendent to them – a separate entity. The two conceptions cannot be easily reconciled.

Turning to manifestations of the self, Jung is consistent: they are essentially symbolic and represent opposites. So it becomes difficult to develop a satisfactory theory of the self because any statement about it can be contradicted – at least this is the notion of its symbolic nature as commonly interpreted. It is consequently held that the self is an ultimate mystery and little attempt need be made to try and elucidate it. In relating the self both empirically and in theory to religious experience, and in particular to knowledge of God, Jung certainly brought the self into relation with theological speculation about ultimate reality. I shall make no attempt to consider this aspect of his work: it is almost completely irrelevant to maturation processes in childhood and this field belongs to philosophy and theology anyway. There are plenty of aspects of the self that we know little or nothing about and its real nature is obscure enough without hypostatising the sense of mystery which ought, in my view, to act as a stimulus to further enquiry rather than an end in itself.

That the self conceived as an ultimate mystery is at

variance with the idea that its realisation is the aim of individuation cannot be gainsaid, for to be realised it must be knowable; but it is often observed that its realisation involves a sense of its mystery.

It was later in the growth of his ideas that Jung developed a different idea: the self was an organiser, the central archetype. The revised concept covered some of his data very well, but it obviously modifies or even does away with the totality concept since the self is conceived as one of its parts. In my view the contradiction can be met by recognising that two levels of abstraction are involved. The totality concept of the self is based on an abstraction from the data which are grouped as symbols or representations of the self: each of these is incomplete but summated they lead to the totality theory. The self as an organiser of the archetypes is less abstract, nearer to the data and, one may say, less theoretical.

How far the concepts developed by Jung and others have been used, developed or discarded by me will appear from subsequent chapters. It may, however, be anticipated that the model of the ego, the archetypes and the self will stand, as also will the relevance of parents in relation to child development and psychopathology. Symbolic imagery and the inner world on which Jung laid so much emphasis, though partly as a compensation for its frequent denial, will also find an important place.

I have given much prominence to the self defined as the organised totality of conscious and unconscious systems. The conception applied to the child treats him as an entity in himself from which the maturational processes can be derived. It does not include mother or the family. The significance of postulating a primary unity will become apparent but perhaps it may be said here that it is conceived as the basis on which the sense of personal identity rests and from which individuation proceeds.

From this position the ideal aim of parents may be defined as fostering maturation of the self and so facilitating the child's sense of self-reliance in relation to them, his siblings and the larger environment into which he progressively embarks as time goes on.

So far nothing has been said about the numerous psychoanalysts to whom reference will be made in the following chapters. They have not, except of course for Freud, anteceded my own endeavours in the same sense as the work of

Jung and Wickes, because I was not working with psychoanalytic theories in the first place and have had no formal training in psychoanalysis.

However, in the early years I gained special stimulus from Klein's pioneering in the psychoanalysis of children; her play techniques which revolutionised child psychotherapy in Great Britain were especially important. Many of her theoretical formulations furthermore struck me even in 1935 as being compatible with Jung's ideas. Her concept of unconscious fantasy and of good and bad objects seemed, for instance, designed to be incorporated into the theory of archetypes and the opposites; in addition early conflict situations such as the violence of the infant's aggressive attacks on his mother's body were, I thought, analogous to the mythological theme of the hero in strife with monsters, as I noted in 1944 in the first edition of this book. I have also come to accept the importance of the depressive position.

That other psychoanalysts, apparently independently, have introduced concepts of the self and its representations into their conceptual thinking, and that individuation has become accepted as a feature of maturation (c.f. Mahler et al. 1975) could not fail to be of great interest to me. Perhaps, however, it will make for increased understanding if I add a remark on the fruitful dialogue between the two schools of analytical psychology and psychoanalysis that has gone on over the years in London. It has contributed to much of my work and that of other members of the London Society of Analytical Psychology. This dialogue could not, however, have taken place without continuing study of Jung's work nor without personal correspondence and discussion with him and Mrs Jung up to the time of their deaths. This gave me a reliable base on which to depend and from which to launch out into new fields of investigation.

2 PLAY

Play, though not the first, is a very early activity of infants. As soon as the breast becomes an object and when mouthing has become a pleasure apart from sucking, play with the nipple and with other parts of the mother has started. It continues when the breast is not available and when hunger and thirst are satisfied, in the exercise of muscles, gurgling, making noises and the like.

Given security provided first by the mother's holding or less direct forms of care (for instance in provision of a cot or play pen) other objects can be explored as well as the nipple and the breast. Gradually it comes about that the mother's face, mouth, hair and parts of the child's own body, his toes, fingers, excreta and genital organs are drawn into his exploratory play. Later this process becomes part of the infant's method of developing his relation to himself and the outside world. It also assists in organising imaginative activity brought about by processes in the self.

Related to the body, play is an early ego activity which happens first when the infant is in a state near to integration. Assuming that in play the infant ego is near to the self, play may be expected to form representations of the self. To put it another way, in early play the infant is making a first step from being a self to finding himself.

Of particular interest are the transitional phenomena whose investigation we owe to Winnicott (1958 and 1967). They will be discussed later on in more detail. Here it need only be said that early in the infant's life he becomes occupied with bits of material or other primitive objects which come to represent neither his 'inner' world nor a bit of his mother who represents the 'outer' world. The transitional phenomena are thus held to occupy a place between the inner and outer worlds of the growing infant. As development proceeds the object acquires, from the infant's point of view, a life and vitality of its own, but its content gradually diffuses till it becomes '. . . not so much forgotten as relegated to limbo . . .'. It loses its energy content because, as Winnicott holds, the transitional phenomena become diffused, spread out over the whole intermediate territory between 'inner psychic reality' and the 'external world as perceived by two persons in common' (1958, p.233). Thus it is the forerunner of the meaningful element in play with many objects but it can also become a fantasy, an image or a thought (infra p.139), and these, if Winnicott is correct, lie at the root of cultural life. This view has its own forerunners, for Harrison states (1927, p.17, fn.4), 'a child's toys in antiquity were apt to be much more than mere playthings. They were charms inductive of good, prophylactic against evil influences'; but attractive as it is, it has not been sufficiently substantiated.

In amplification of the concept it is a common observation that children treat some objects as essential to their well-being: they become endowed with meaning and cannot be taken away without vigorous objections. They are the toys, usually soft dolls, teddy bears and the like, that children carry about with them, take to bed, or are special and preferred before all others. Besides being special objects one characteristic of these objects is their 'objectiveness'. A child may refer to events in his outer or inner worlds, indeed sometimes transparently so, but all the same the play is itself considered as the results of diffusion, an 'objective' activity.

In what I have said and in what follows, it is no object of mine to develop a general theory of play. I rather want to indicate the characteristics which a clinician or one closely involved with children may find useful. During psychotherapy the following features are worth bearing in mind:

1. Through the small size of toys the child has, within the limits imposed by the nature of the toy, complete control over his play; so there is ample scope for expressing and enjoying valuable feelings of omnipotence, especially when expressed in creative play with the primary materials, water, sand, plasticine, clay, and in painting and drawing.

2. Omnipotent play can be autoerotic, and then it is carried on alone: the rewards are its own and the child does not require anybody else to appreciate what is being done. This play can also be creative: it is where symbols are often found.

3. Usually, however, creative play requires appreciation by others, and especially parents; if this is not provided the child may become sad or even depressed, angry or despairing.

4. This leads on to play as a vehicle for meaningful communication, the element which has proved especially useful to analysts. Instead of talking, the child will play, expressing his loves and hates, hopes and fears, sometimes in a transparent but mostly in a concealed way.

5. As part of this communicative element other people can get drawn into a game by being asked to play roles. At first this activity is self-centred, i.e. the child wants the other person to play a role that represents a part of the self. Later a to-and-fro interchange is possible, and compromises are made. Still later organised games can begin, and these will become the increasingly complex ones of adult life: play has then become social.

The following examples illustrate these features of play – though its creativeness will be taken up later in Chapter 4 – and are designed to show different degrees of organisation at two age periods.

CASE 1 – INFANTILE JEALOUSY AND ENVY

Joyce, aged six years, suffered from fears of the dark, and a school phobia.

First Interview:
She seemed a lively, active little girl, full of energy which she found at times difficult, or impossible, to control, and when this happened she became anxious.

Play: She started to play with two dolls, one black and the other white. The black doll was 'bad' and was smacked a lot on her bare 'behind', after which she was put to bed. Later this doll was given some nice clothes and in the end Joyce became more reconciled to her. The other doll, called 'the baby', was good and much loved. On one occasion, when both children were in bed together, Joyce discovered that the good baby's eyes would not close. At first she '*could not* go to sleep'. Later it appeared that she *would not* do so, and a mild argument ensued in which the 'good baby' was called 'naughty'.

In this game Joyce played at being mother, dressing and undressing the children, smacking one, caressing the other, and putting them both to bed: this is normal play. At six years of age identification of a little girl with her mother is to be expected, and is usual as part of her oedipal conflict. That each doll develops as part of itself a germ of the opposite quality shows this is near to whole object play: the 'bad child' is put into nice clothes, probably as a reward for being good, though there has been no real change in her nature, as subsequent play showed; the 'good' child has a bit of 'badness' within her in the form of the deliberate intention not to close her eyes and go to sleep.

As a whole the child's play was dominated by remorseless punitive acts, all directed to controlling 'bad' behaviour. The violence is evidently an attempt to control her bad infantile wishes which she fears. Because of her tendency to ruthlessness there is evidence that her identification with the mother is part of a residual manic defence (c.f. infra p.195). Her fantasy-mother does not correspond to the real behaviour of the child's own mother towards her, for the child was her favourite. This suggests that projective and introjective identifications contribute to the picture she presents (c.f. infra p.76).

Second Interview:

There was a good deal of playing with water, using a small tin bath with a reservoir attached; by turning on a tap the water ran into the bath. The tap, however, became blocked and this upset Joyce. Later on she put some boats in a large tray into which she poured water from a bucket; she pushed the boats to and fro in it. She also put a lot of sand in the water and when she got her hands wet complained that they would get chapped. Then she wanted the water changed to separate the sand and water, and together we carried a bucket up and down stairs, splashing it about as we did so.

In this play there is a tendency to pair objects: there are two boats, the sand and the water go together, the tap which ejects water and the bath which contains it. Dealing, however, with materials and impersonal objects, there is more reality in what she does and no need to distinguish between good and bad.

Third Interview:
The bad doll was once again well beaten and put in the corner at the beginning of the interview. After this there was much play with water; Joyce was mother washing the doll's clothes and bedclothes. Whilst washing the knickers with soap she got some sand on them. This she smelt because she thought it was 'busy' (faeces), but when she discovered that the 'busy' was sand she was content. She also washed the floor carefully and made me move my chair about so as to let her get on with the work. At one time when she was washing she came across some drops of water on the floor. 'That's baby's "tidly" [urine] down there. She got out of bed and came downstairs and did "tidly"; she's a nuisance, naughty baby,' she said.

Sand play: She made a 'dumpling' and cooked it.

Tea party: She was mother making tea and I was daddy. Suddenly she said, 'My baby's crying,' and took off the nappies. When she smelt 'busy', she said, 'She's a pest. Busying on knickers.'

The identification with the mother is once again clear, but this time Joyce's actions are more closely related to reality and reflect her real mother's behaviour, washing and cooking whilst many of her remarks, 'She's a pest,' for example, are ones that her mother actually makes. The theme of the play has also changed in that the baby had become less good. Her badness, suggested in the earlier interview when she would not shut her eyes, has now extended to anal activities. In relation to these Joyce is less ruthless than before probably since the 'bad' doll has been got rid of. She spends her time at the beginning in making everything clean. This leads to the discovery of dirt: 'busy'. By referring to reality, i.e. by discovering that the 'busy' is sand, she checks her anger; other activities are treated with severity but no punishment.

Fourth Interview:
Joyce found the baby's bottle and enjoyed sucking and chewing the teat. Early in the interview she commented, 'My baby can spit back.' This means that the baby spat the milk out. For this she was spanked.

Soon after she found some chalks which she broke up and put in a little tray for chalks fixed to a blackboard. After this she said, 'Is she crying? Is my baby crying?' and went to feed her. 'Does she spit it out?' she said, and then sucked the bottle herself. Some water ran out from the wrong end, and she cried, 'Oh tidly!' Then she bit and chewed the teat. 'Been to see our Uncle Alf's baby,' she said. She spilt more water on the floor. At this I remarked, 'When you were a baby perhaps you wanted to do tidly over mum just like you spill water on the floor now.' To this she replied, 'No, I didn't, but I used to do busy all over her – you can't smack babies.' She then put the bottle down. 'I'm going to save it for tonight,' and she found a toy bath that was dirty – to her disgust. She put some water in it, washed some soldiers, commenting on their guns, and put them in a wastepaper basket. She then found another bath with 'muck' in it. 'A boy put it in last night.' Next she said, 'I must make haste and get my daddy's dinner, then I can put the bath on the tap.' She was near an electric switch screwed to the wall; 'I want this,' she said, and took the loose screw out. Next she tried to open the door of a cupboard, but the key would not work and she struggled to make the door open. I offered to help her, but she refused. 'Oh no, oh no, oh no,' she said; then, 'What are you crying for, baby? Naughty!'

She next found paint and a brush and pretended to be sick. She went and took sand out of the sand tray, sprinkling it all over the floor. She found the baby doll, picked it up and gave it the bottle. In doing so she spilt water all over the ground. At once she smacked the baby, next found its pants wet and smacked it again: 'She's a pest.' Next the bottle became 'a pest', and she sucked and bit it.

There are many new features in this play. In the first place the identification with mother is not so strong and for much of the interview she works out her feelings of being a baby: actually doing babyish things, sucking and chewing the teat of the bottle. But not all of them are safe to act out for they are punishable, so she projects her feelings into the doll and punishes her. For the first time there is no rejection of the black doll and though there are some hard words and sound smacks for the 'baby', her behaviour is on the whole less obsessive, more violent but tends to become restless.

Taking the play as a whole the sequence suggests that the 'bad' things in the black doll represented the split off behaviour of the good baby, and as the baby gets worse the black doll is less 'bad'. Though 'mother' tries to force the baby to give up her dirty ways by punishment, this does not apply to herself as a baby, for when she brings out her desire to do 'busy' all over her mother she at once protects herself by the opinion 'mustn't smack babies'. However, when she feels like it she soon sets about the 'baby' who is no longer herself.

The arrest in development, which must be assumed to have been inflexible because of her fears, centres round the persistence of baby wishes and her ruthless wish for punishment to keep them under control. By creating a tolerant situation in which the play can take place Joyce could work out her conflicts. The objects which Joyce used most were: the black and white dolls; the bottle, standing at one time for the breast which she bites, at another for the body from which pours 'tidly'; sand and water, which represent 'busy' and 'tidly'.

Once her pre-oedipal conflicts are ventilated she brings forward her feelings about sexual differences. For example, all phallic objects are either attacked or thrown away, whilst boys are stated to be dirty. Chalks are broken, the soldiers with their guns are put in the wastepaper basket and she is disgusted by a paint brush and is sick over it.

Considering the play as a whole, the way Joyce reacts to serious frustration is very obvious. First she is ruthless and tries to overcome it by force, refusing all help; but other less impetuous methods are there as well, represented in the form of a question, 'What are you crying for, baby?'

In later interviews, as the play went on its violence increased till she threw the baby on the fire, and after this climax she became more moderate and showed more concern. It is now not difficult to understand why Joyce cannot go to school. Throughout the play the 'mother's' brutality is clearly seen. Since her mother is not in reality like this, the brutal mother archetype becomes projected on to the schoolmistress, whom she cannot overcome and in whose presence she is overcome by helpless, frightened and tearful feelings.

Conclusion:

These play episodes represent a common feature of development: a little girl's envy and jealousy at the arrival of a younger brother. It occurred during the period in which her oedipal conflict was in evidence and her identification with her mother derived largely from this period. However, concurrently there has been a regression expressed in her infantile manic and so defensive violence. Her attempts to solve her anxieties by regression and by identification with the baby have not been successful, for the ruthlessness of her play and tendency to treat the babies as good *or* bad, not both, lands her in a position which cannot be sustained because she has developed far enough to recognise that one person can be good *and* bad.

Some bits of the play point to other features of the oedipal phase. There are rather clear castration anxieties and penis envy is hinted at, whilst very remotely suggested are interest and anxieties about the primal scene (c.f. infra p.101).

There is in this play also a feature of some cultural interest. The good and bad objects (babies) seem confused and there is a tendency of one to turn into the other; but though the good baby has bad characteristics and the bad one good features they never refer to one and the same person. For opposites to behave in this way is a typical state of affairs: Jung called it 'enantiodromia'. Their intermixing is characteristic not only of Joyce's but of many children's play and is reflected in cultural forms. The relation was a special concern of alchemists in contrast to dogmatic aspects of Christianity, but the most organised expression of enantiodromia is found in Chinese philosophy. The Great Monad is a standard 'diagram' used probably for meditation. It depicts two fishes, one representing Yang, the other Yin, each being the same size as the other and containing within it a germ of its opposite. The monad infers a phasic relation of the two; when Yang predominates Yin is recessive, and vice versa. This principle has been applied to the whole of nature and to the history of nations.

The cultural significance of Joyce's play is thus that she is expressing in a direct, simple, flexible form the pattern of a dynamic system which has been abstracted, refined, meditated upon and developed into a complex philosophical idea.

CASE 2 – A FIXATION TO THE FATHER

The following record of play of a girl, Joan, aged ten and a half years, is selected from a long series of her records extending over a year. Whilst away from home she had become a profuse bed-wetter. She had always been enuretic, but only slightly, so that when she returned her bed-wetting again ceased to be serious. She was born in India and came to England when she was four years old. Two years later her father deserted the family, leaving them practically destitute. Joan had pleasant memories of her father and his desertion came as a severe blow, expressed in her feeling that she would never get married when she grew up because it opened up the possibility that she, like her mother, would be left by her husband.

Early on in her play therapy Joan told me two of her dreams.

Dream 1

A bomb fell in the back yard and I put my head on my arm waiting for the explosion that would kill me. Mother went out and put earth on it and a flowerpot over it out of which grew a flower.

Joan's mother is here shown to be a good one, converting destructive affects into a positive form.

Dream 2

(Joan related this after coming to the clinic for some weeks.) My father had come back again. He was married to Mrs Wood and was packing his bags before coming to see us.

Joan was overjoyed by this dream and told it to her family. Her mother, no doubt pleased with it herself, said, 'Perhaps you will find daddy on the doorstep when you go out!' but her sister expressed the more cynical, 'When you dream of a thing it never comes true!'

In reply to a question, Joan said that she had only caught a glimpse of her father and could not be at all sure what he looked like. Mrs Wood, she said, 'lives next door and has a large family'.

Since this dream was told soon after she came to the clinic it is fair to assume that she has already begun to transfer her feelings to me. I have begun to seem like the father she remembered and so a situation is already being created in which she may resume the development broken by her father's desertion. Her play may give clues about her ability to deal with this problem. She will not in reality have her mother with her, so that the explosive, destructive effects of the first dream are likely to come in as well as positive elements which live 'next door'.

Chasing games

As soon as she had got used to the clinic she began a series of chasing games. She would run away as fast as she could, inviting me to chase her; she would run till I was 'lost', and then she would hide, expecting me to find her. If she was caught she would surrender for a moment with some pleasure, but would then use this surrender to escape again. She here shows her ambivalent, provocative, seductive and anxious feelings, probably related to the violence of her sexual fears. In this testing-out play she is evidently relating to the dark side of her father expressed in the dream of the bomb.

At times she would give up the chasing game and start others, cutting up paper and mixing it with bits of grass to make a 'poison pie'.

Ball games

When Joan began to play with a ball her games changed. At first she bounced it on the ground or against the wall, catching it on the rebound. Later she included me in the game, not allowing me, however, to catch the ball by throwing it far away; once up towards the sun, saying that I should not catch it unless it was 'in front of the sun'. Then she went on to make other conditions, such as that I must not catch it before it bounced. Lastly she began a game of rounders, setting up four posts round which to run. During this part of the play there was no conflict about who should have the ball since there were standard rules of the organised game.

The sequences of ball games ended with rounders. It is a formal game in which there are four poles, one of which is 'home', from which you start and to which you return. In the game she could express her antagonism and competition with me more easily – she need not fear attack because the rules of the game are reliable. This condition did not last for long; nor would it be expected to.

The social element in this game hardly needs underlining. However, the form of the game is a mandala which combines two symbolic elements. According to Jung four is a number which expresses opposites in a stable or complete relation to each other; the idea of facing a problem represents this stability. Rounders, as its name implies, also involves a circle, a widespread symbol expressing anything from defensive magic to a perfect form.

Supposing the child chose the four posts unconsciously to express her equivalent of these ideas, it could follow that she and I personify previously warring but now complementary functions in safe rivalry.

The symbolism of the ball game seemed to express the

greater sense of security Joan felt, indeed once it began her anxiety was temporarily mastered, as the symbolism of it would require, since a mandala represents a stable integrate. This state implies that a different focus of her conflicts would now come to the fore.

Water games

The next group of games centred round the use of water. Joan first became attracted to it by watching a boy playing with a hose-pipe. She tried to obstruct the flow of water by treading on it; to this the boy objected and when she persisted he grew annoyed. Joan then went and turned the water off at the tap, but the boy turned it on again and a game ensued in which her rival tried to keep the water running whilst Joan tried to stop it. Later, while the boy was turning on the tap, she picked up the hose and turned the water on to the boy. At one time during these activities Joan wanted to go to the lavatory and in subsequent play the relation between the flow of water and going to the lavatory was particularly noticeable.

In other interviews Joan used the water for different purposes, such as watering the garden or filling up a small concrete pond. At times when she was watering the garden she would find cracks in the ground (it was during a very dry summer); she would concentrate on these and appear to drive the water into the earth, assuming as she did so a brutal look. In one of the interviews she became very excited and sprayed the water on a female therapist who was present at the time. Spraying other people extended to spraying me, calling me 'rubbish' as she did so, and also the boy and the woman. In her excitement she would get very imperious.

Joan's play with the hose and with water thus brought with it changes of mood – a passive vacant unconsciousness when she filled the pond, a brutal concentration when she watered into the cracks, an imperious excitement when she attacked people, a more or less neutral state when she watered the garden.

In this play Joan's sexuality came more into the open. Her rivalry with the boy implied her penis envy, her wish to attack his penis and to possess one of her own. Her activities brought the instinctual root of her bed-wetting to the fore. There seemed to be fantasies of intercourse very near the surface: she conceived it as fierce and brutal and, if this were correct, in her play she would be trying out mostly male but also possible female roles. I therefore interpreted her acts and feelings to her and she immediately turned the water once again on to the female therapist, showing less inhibition, less excitement and more control in her activity. These changes suggested that my intervention had been valuable in reducing her anxiety.

School games

The next series of games centred on school. In these she invariably played the part of teacher at the blackboard, teaching spelling and sums. Various problems which arose at school came into her game, in which she was evidently imitating the real teacher: I took part in the game by acting as Joan's pupil, expressing verbally some of the protests which I expected she felt and would like to have expressed in school. Daydreaming was one of them, boredom another, pleasure at getting sums right, and also complaints about the teacher. To any form of 'naughtiness' she reacted at first with verbal violence and later with threats of physical punishment.

This is like Joyce's play in the severity of the disapproval and punishments: once again the play is ruthless and – like Joyce's – not related to reality. In each case the child is working out her fear of sadistic punishment by identification but in Joan the aggressive impulses and fantasies are clearly moving forward and related to more mature genital organisation.

The shadow personality

One day Joan began to play with a puzzle, which she set out to complete. The puzzle was easy and she certainly could have done it if she wished but she tired of it and referred to 'me and the person that can do this puzzle'. She has split herself into two.

She then went to a blackboard and drew a picture (Drawing I). First she made a dotted outline and asked me what I thought it was. I suggested that it was a shadow of a person, a ghost. At once she began to elaborate the parts of the figure, and as she did so, I asked her about it. Why the big ears? They felt like that, she said, when her mother shouted at her. What about the two faces? 'Oh that is because I talk to myself.' Soon after this she wrote on the board, 'Dr. Fordham's ghost', and then a riotous game ensued – sometimes fleeing from the 'Dr. Fordham ghost',

Drawing I 'The Shadow Personality' (copy of the original)

sometimes violently attacking him with threats, 'beatings', tyrannical behaviour and inhibited attempts at biting. Eventually she ordered me to stand on the lawn and not move.

When, later on, I asked her about ghosts she told me that there were good ones and bad ones. The good ones were kind to her, i.e. they were like her memories of her father.

Joan's behaviour then illustrates two ways of dealing with an object of fear: she runs away and identifies with it. That she runs away is clear, but what evidence is there of identification? In the first place she becomes cruel and brutal and uses her mouth with which to bite. Since it is this side of her which she fears to express, her actions may safely be taken as a manifestation of her defensive counter-phobic identification; in terms of fantasy she has been devoured by the 'ghost' and uses its form of attack (c.f. also Picture IV, p.61). The identification, however, is transient, and she makes it objective by projection on to me, then she separates from it by defining a place where it can be confined and controlled.

From now on, though some playful chasing occurred, there

was a further change in Joan's play. A long series of games followed in which she became a mother looking after her babies, seeing a child off to school, cooking, sending imaginary children on errands, keeping the house 'nice' and 'bad people' out of it. These make it certain that Joan had worked through her identification with the negative image of her father and had established her oedipal identifications with her mother.

An early memory

Once she played that she and I went for a long journey in a train lasting three days. The phrase 'three days' referred to India, so I asked Joan what memories she had of those times, and she told me that one day her grandfather saw a snake's head coming under the door of their house. Her father and grandfather killed the animal.

My object in citing this memory is to illustrate how play is related to the past as well as the present. The dramatic action of much play is indicative of, but also conceals, the more simple and often painful realities.

Much of Joan's play is dramatising how she felt about her father when she was small. The memory, in contrast to the others, is of his violence in reality, and I assumed that she wanted to tell me through her memory that his, and so her violence also, was defensive and not usually in evidence.

A COMPARISON OF THE TWO CHILDREN'S PLAY

A comparison of these two children's play reveals many points of similarity. In each there is the same problem of using rules and regulations, the same tendency to punish and reject what is bad. In each case the play is used to work through and master anxieties which could not be managed in everyday life, and in each case the source of anxiety was unintegrated, aggressive and libidinal drives and the fantasies connected with them. It is these functions of play as a whole which make it therapeutic, particularly when tolerance is shown by adult persons.

The differences may be summed up as follows: Joan showed greater deliberation and capacity to understand what she did; there was less spontaneous direct reaction, less concern purely with home life and more with school. She has indeed a greater width of outlook, and though primitive infantile affects are there, they are only expressed after working through better established defences. In short her ego is the stronger of the two because she is older.

A NOTE ON SOCIAL PLAY

The children's play that has been recorded and discussed led in the direction of organised games which feature so much in educational systems and cultural life. They have features of sufficient psychological interest to warrant a short note about them.

In all games there is a conflict between two 'sides', each composed of one person, or when a stated number each individual takes his part in a group opposed to the 'other side'. The two contesting groups are exactly the same numerically and arranged in the same way, but each side has an emotional tone attached to it; one side is positive, 'our' side, the other side is negative, 'their' side; and it is from these opposites that the activity of the game develops.

The essential opposition of psychological processes is therefore expressed in the game, whose aim is for our 'good' side to win. The individual, being a member of the side, may be thought of as representing the ego conceived as part only of the whole psyche which contains within it many other figures of equal or greater potency arranged in opposites. Each side aims at winning and usually but not always a definitive result is achieved. It is characteristic of children that they identify themselves with one 'our side', which represents the best side and so represents the 'good' people externally and internally the good or superior objects.

These characteristics make organised games a particularly suitable field for the expression of emotional states, and so enthusiasm for games is often more common than is enthusiasm for 'work'. Games can, however, be played in various ways, in different spirits, and the spirit of games links up with the spirit of community in which the games are played. But in all of them ideas of fair play, of being able to take a beating, and of appreciating the beaten side, are rooted deep in the structure of our society.

If there is one thing which makes for mental health it is the realisation that one is part of a whole both psychically and socially, and that there is at the same time always a side which though inferior needs to be given its place. The largest part of analytical work is concerned with bringing the inferior or shadow (i.e. 'their') side up into consciousness – and the difficulties of doing so derive from its having been forced out of consciousness through excessive development of one side of the personality. In games this would be equivalent to overcoming the other side by unfair methods such as cheating and crippling one or more of its members. Thus games provide an illustration of how the collective life plays upon deepseated psychological processes and represents them in consciousness thus mitigating against unrealistic attitudes.

3 Dreams

Amplification is undoubtedly the most sophisticated method that Jung developed to elucidate the meaning of dreams. Since dreams can reveal myth-like imagery and some of them a story-like quality, amplification can and has been applied to them, and by this means it is easy to show that archetypal forms are active in early childhood. Parent figures are frequent and the shadow, the animus, the anima and the self-representations (c.f. infra p.71) can be found long before the onset of adolescence.

To have established analogies between a child's dream and complex mythological forms was a significant achievement at a time when it was beginning to be understood that the behaviour and play of small children indicated the influence of very primitive unconscious fantasies in the first months of life. It made for greater confidence in applying the theory of archetypes to the study not only of childhood but also of infancy.

Jung, however, with characteristic daring, pushed his theory of the archetypes and the collective unconscious to conclusions to which, as I have already suggested, few can follow him.

Children's dreams clearly made a great impression on him: 'Many of them', he writes, 'are very simple "childish" dreams and are immediately understandable, but others contain possibilities of meaning that almost make one's head spin, and things that reveal their profound significance only in the light of primitive parallels . . . Dreams and images appear before the soul of the child, shaping his whole destiny as well as those retrospective intuitions which reach back far beyond the range of childhood experience into the life of our ancestors' (C.W.8, p.52).

Though Jung modified his position in later publications this passage suggests that archetypal dreams in childhood support the idea of there being a cultural heritage which is not transmitted by parents and teachers but which is accessible to a child *a priori*. The child's inheritance is, he continues, 'highly differentiated . . . and consists of mnemonic deposits accruing from all the experience of our ancestors' (ibid., p.53).

These passages from Jung, and others like them, have had much influence and have tended to focus attention away from the analysis of dreams in terms of the child himself. It is here that the use of amplification can and has led to adultomorphic speculation, a phrase meaning that adult characteristics are wrongly attributed to children. As a consequence the way to understanding children is blocked. The tendency to seize on to interesting dreams and fantasies and relate them to social, mythical forms can become irresistible and has led to forgetting that the images are ones which the child has developed. In this volume the idea has already been introduced that a child does not inherit from birth a culture to be revealed in dreams as Jung's formulation implies. Having rejected Jung's extreme position, from which he later withdrew, the whole question still needs sorting out. Without doubt there is a cultural element and signs of it can be observed in child behaviour, thoughts, fantasies and dreams. The controversial issue centres round how this state of affairs can be explained. There are three ways of approaching the subject:

1. It can be held that the whole cultural heritage is transmitted in the genes. There is nothing in favour of this proposition. Only the archetypes themselves are inherited and even this has not been proved, though it was Jung's later position and the one I adhere to myself.

2. The cultural heritage is transmitted by parents and teachers who induct the child progressively into the traditional values of the society in which he is to live.

3. The child himself works out patterns of behaviour, thought and fantasy, as part of maturation. He uses at first primitive and later increasingly refined thought processes to discover what is valid for them, then adapting them to the requirements of society as he discovers its structure.

In the following pages I shall apply these formulations to elucidate, if not find an answer to them, by studying first what is known of the dreams of infants and how they develop in early childhood; next by elucidating a striking dream having patently mythical characteristics, and finally by using Jung's dream series technique to see whether other evidence can be adduced to gain further understanding of the issue.

DREAMS IN INFANCY

There can be no doubt that dream processes start very early in life, indeed it is known that REM rhythms can be recorded in the brain during intra-uterine life. Since these are closely correlated with dreaming, it must be supposed that there is some sort of dream process active then. Though what such a dream can be like is hard to imagine. Infant observation of sleeping infants also indicates disturbances which may well be caused by dreams.

The following is an example of an infant dreaming:

For some time a boy aged nine months had been waking up at night and was to be found clinging excitedly to his cot. His mother resourcefully discovered that if she took down the side of the cot and lifted the infant in the direction he seemed to be looking, the child regularly ended up underneath the cot. After this he would go back to sleep. From this dramatic sequence the mother concluded that he saw a moving object going in this direction and that the activities were the continuation of a dream.

The child had recently started eating solids and was given, amongst other foods, some fish. With the fish he had connected a sound which he used during the excitement he manifested. At about the same time he awoke crying during his rest period in the garden and in his tears he made the same sound. His mother inferred from this and other signs that he had dreamt of something like fish biting him.

DREAMS OF EARLY CHILDHOOD

Observations of this kind are rarely recorded and as far as I know no systematic studies have been made of dreams during infancy. In later years many data have been collected and, indeed, once a small child can play, the content of his dreams can be inferred by correlating sleep disturbances with his behaviour, as the following example illustrates. A little girl aged just three years of age was suffering from night terrors.

In her interviews with me she at first showed manifest anxiety in leaving her mother and started a series of games in which biting various objects featured as a central theme. As the games became more and more violent, the night terrors diminished and eventually ceased.

It will be noticed that biting featured in the dreams of both the little girl and the baby who was in the process of being weaned. Bearing in mind the important place taken by very primitive fantasies that happen concurrently with biting the breast in infancy, the infant and the young child are likely to have been in the process of representing their oral attacks on the breast or derivatives of it. Each in his own way had become terrified of a danger felt as real and physical because object and fantasy were not yet distinguished.

The observation that early dreams of children are often connected with biting has been confirmed and generalised by study of pre-school children. Despert, for instance, collected 190 dreams from thirty-nine children between two and five years of age. To do this, little dolls and beds of a suitable size were provided and also a real couch and a pillow. Since speech was not usually sufficiently developed, the child could reply to questions or would spontaneously communicate dreams by dramatic action using the play material.

By employing this technique Despert arrived at the following conclusions. The earliest dreams of two-year-olds are associated with the three statements: 'Chase me . . .', 'Bite me . . .', 'Eat me up . . .', but no mention is made of 'the how or who' is acting. Between the ages of three and five the agent has become specific: it is always an animal and further the animal is a real one – a dog, a bear, a tiger and the like – derived from the immediate domestic environment or from animals mentioned and seen in pictures. These observations suggest that the primary imagery of a small child's dreams is realistic. After two years other themes appear, such as attacks on a baby brother. Only by three to four years have ghosts and witches been recorded. At about five, there are people who 'are frequently destructive, superhuman in size and power and sometimes supernatural' (Despert 1949, p.161). The elements of fire and water are common and particularly interesting is the fact, to which we may refer later, that with only one exception parents do not appear in hostile, aggressive or destructive roles. Thus by five years of age quite a wide range of themes has developed.

These conclusions suggest that the pattern known later in mythology as the devouring animal mother starts very early as, indeed, would be expected, and originates in the projection of violent fantasies which accompany early feeding experiences and the frustration of oral drives.

DREAMS AFTER FIVE YEARS

It seems easy to elicit dreams from small children, but later on it can become difficult. Sophisticated attitudes develop, often reflecting those of their parents, which facilitate, obstruct or distort communication. Some children talk freely about their dreams, others 'never have them', whilst again others suppress them altogether or particular parts of them; lastly there are those who invent them. And so it becomes important to consider how they are collected as well as what they are like.

Dream series

Two series of dreams from a boy, John, and a girl, Jane, were collected by their mother. She herself had a lively and serious interest in them derived from analytic experience of her own. Knowing this the two children started telling their own dreams and so a dialogue developed which became part of their everyday family life. Usually in the morning the two children told their dreams to their mother and exchanged thoughts and reflections about them. The interchange went on for about three years and was sustained by my interest in it, for the mother came and discussed them with me on a friendly basis. A factor in collecting this unusually long series, comprising over 200 dreams, was the mother's need for help because of the depression which followed her husband's death when the younger child was a baby. That the study of dreams led to analysis of the mother is perhaps not altogether surprising, but I have no reason to think that this influenced her special relation to the children over the actual dreaming itself, nor that her psychopathology influenced significantly the telling of them, nor the content of what the children said. All the dreams are of the kind that would be expected of children and they were not obviously elaborated by fantasy.

This series suggests strongly that whether children tell dreams or no is largely dependent upon the attitude of those in their immediate environment. It contrasts with the idea that children do not talk about nor report their dreams, because they develop a reticence that is inherent in child development. Dreams, it is held, become part of the child's secret inner world into which parents may not enter. That this view is at fault is supported by the fact that school children enjoy telling or writing their dreams down as part of a free exercise period. Alternatively they may be made into a subject matter for essay-writing.

In line with the idea that whether children tell dreams or not depends on the real or imagined interest that the adults in their immediate environment have in them, are observations in the series of dreams to be studied later in this chapter. They were obtained from a child coming to see me for therapeutic interviews. At that time I myself had a special interest in dreams and so repeatedly stimulated him to tell them by asking about them at the first interview, continuing to suggest he tell me one when he was at a loss for something to do or talk about. He enjoyed them and I exploited his pleasure. By contrast since I have applied analytic techniques to child therapy and do not press children to tell them, dreams feature less. When they are communicated they are told as part of the total situation and so related to play, to fantasy, and to other verbal communications. This procedure has facilitated the analysis of a dream with a child, but leads to many dreams not being told.

To collect dreams by a method which exploits the child's feelings about his therapist is useful because understanding of the dream in itself is worthwhile, or perhaps I might say was worthwhile when I was using it. Study of dreams in this fashion facilitates understanding of preconscious processes but does not help in penetrating into the more unconscious ones. The method has, however, disadvantages, one of which it is appropriate to consider now. With very few exceptions it has been observed that the mother appears only in a positive role, even when this is in defiance of reality. Even children who by adult and their own standards are badly treated by their parents have only good dreams about their own mothers. The bad mother images are nearly always mythologised as witches, ghosts, animals and the like. The evidence of the two children is interesting in this respect.

Examination of the ninety-five dreams in the collection told by John shows that his mother appears forty times. She is helpful, comforting, idealised, giving education, mediating or passive. When she is absent it is known where she has gone; sometimes she is wanted in her absence. When she is frustrating it is mild; sometimes she is as much the victim of dangers as the children. There was one exception and that was when, in a dream, she killed herself. The same applies to Jane's series, so the difference in sex does not affect the result.

Now the mother was a good enough mother in spite of her depression and the need to substitute the memory of her husband by focusing her libidinal investment on her children. She was creative, helpful, and seldom if ever directed uncontrolled or violent aggression against her children. But she did punish or frustrate them when necessary; there is no hint that these situations became the subject for dreaming.

A clue to this state of affairs was given by a remark made by John. On one occasion he told part of a dream and then said: 'I had another in which Mummy got the bad part, but I can't remember that dream, because I won't let Mummy have the bad part. She should only get the good part in my dream.' To this his elder sister agreed. John was seven years and seven months old at this time and his sister eleven years and four months.

The phenomenon, observed first by Despert, who called it segregation, is general and is due either to deliberate suppression or forgetting. It can be associated with a common feature of childhood. The need to maintain parents as good, and particularly the mother, is clearly seen in that children will not, or cannot, tolerate criticism of their parents by others. It can further be observed during child analysis. If a child is to recognise and assimilate his feeling that one or other of his parents is in some respect bad, it can only be done if the child knows that the analyst recognises that the parent is predominantly good.

This state of affairs probably derives from the child's dependence upon his parents and the original need for his mother to be good enough. In infancy this meant that she was good and *not* bad and if she was not in reality good enough she had to be 'hallucinated' as good. It is this earlier state of affairs that persists in these irrational facts of children's behaviour and dreaming.

Before going on to consider a selection of dreams having manifest archetypal themes in them, it is necessary to state that they are unusual. In the series of 200, Jane told ninety-one, mostly about personal matters relating to school and home. Amongst them there was a group of five 'big dreams', and these will now be studied.

A 'mythological' dream

When Jane was nine years and one month old she was having difficulties in her personal relationships at school. There was nothing very tangible, she did not make enemies and she did not get on badly with teachers, but it was evident and was a sort of absence of something that would be expected of her. The history strongly suggested that this inner state of affairs stemmed from the tragic death of her father when she was very much disturbed. At about the time she told her dream her teacher noted an 'all-round improvement' in her personal relationships and in her work.

'I had a golden baby with a silver star on his forehead. One day I was standing by a river and then an awful thing happened. My baby fell into the river. Then I asked the dragon where she was and he said: "I am going to keep her." Then I stood on a triangle island with trees round about, I had a friend with me. Then some black children came and held hands surrounding the island. Then I said to my friend: "Let's push through the black children." We slipped through. Then I went to the river. I dived down and got my baby.'

This dream is unique in the whole series. It has a beauty and symmetry about it which no other dream possessed. Though there were others communicated at about this time having a myth-like quality, they tailed off into dreams about everyday events. There were one or two isolated ones in later years, echoes of the past, but they never reached this level of perfection. Therefore the group can only represent the culmination of critical changes going on in Jane's inner world.

First to consider the dream as a whole. Its structure and its dynamic pattern depict an integrative–deintegrative–reintegrative sequence (c.f infra pp.87–8 and Chapter 6). The mother–infant unity begins and ends it; the dragon deintegrates into a number of figures: the triangle island with trees and black children and a friend. The baby at first is much idealised; later it becomes 'my baby' and so represents an access of personal feeling that seems to have been won over from the impersonal images.

Next, most of the images, quite apart from the story-like

nature of the dream, are common in fairy stories and myths: the dragon, rivers, trees, magic islands, the star, gold and silver; and the theme of dropping down or going down, usually into the underworld, must be added. Jane's transparent wish to be a mother and possess a baby is idealised through its gold and silver attributes.

Jane had other dreams at this time which can be used to amplify her 'big' dream and show that gold and silver were important to her in varying contexts. One of them occurred when she was nine years and two months old.

'There was a lion called a golden lion, because it had golden paws, but his body was silver. There were two princes, one of my classroom and one of something else. They both wanted to get that golden lion. I pushed the prince from my classroom away saying: "Get the golden lion," and he did get it. He pulled it to my classroom and stood it in front of the blackboard. I stood watching it in wonder. At the same time I was the golden lion. I gave sixpence to it for two days and then I said: "Oh what a pity I have only got fivepence left. This won't do," and then I woke up.'

Soon after this (when she was nine years and three months) she dreamed again of gold and silver.

'Mummy was in the house and John and I were playing in the street with Christopher [a neighbour's boy]. Then God sent daddy down from the sky with lots of gold and silver. He fell into the garden but he did not hurt himself because he was with the good spirits. Then mummy called: "Jane, John, come up quickly and see what is in the garden." Then in half a minute we were in the garden hugging and kissing daddy. Then we went in the house and had a meal.'

Besides showing that gold and silver were important, these dreams suggest the development of concern for her father and her considerable capacity for decisive female activity suggesting on the whole that her aggression was well integrated and her female identity established and reinforced by positive identifications.

The dropping of the baby in the first dream probably refers to the trauma in her life and, indeed, when she was three years old her father died from a heart attack whilst taking her out with him for a walk, and whilst her mother was in hospital after giving birth to John. The last dream introduces death (daddy is in the sky and later 'with the good spirits') and also her wish to have him with the family. These features suggest the culmination of her mourning for him and the grief not only at her own loss but also that which her mother and brother had sustained. In this light the first dream represents a part of her mourning which is now being worked through. The dragon would then represent the negative, possessive, greedy component; also the father and the regressive pull in her grief which had been occupying her and which had appeared from the outside as a defect in her personality.

Pursuing the idea that the island, trees and children are deintegrates of the dragon, the triangle island and the trees would be parts of the father appearing in a more positive light, whilst the 'black children' are the amount of dark infantile feelings previously fused with and now separated from the father, which stand in the way of mastering and working through her negative self-destructive, regressive and greedy grief. And what of the friend: in a general way she shows Jane's good integration of her shadow, and is likely to represent her relation to reality, since the dream ego is introverted. In the second dream her relation to reality is shown by the way she switches from her narcissistic identification with the lion to the realistic recognition, 'I have only got fivepence left. This won't do.'

But there remains consideration of the golden child which it is tempting to approach through intellectual amplification from other sources.

To a mind sophisticated in these subjects there will be no difficulty in perceiving that the baby contains opposites, the silver and gold, whilst the star is the opposite of the body, belonging to the sky as gold belongs to the earth, but this leads us away from Jane herself, though towards the idiom in which she was brought up. Her mother's intense interest in her own symbolic inner world had led her to study the subject extensively, and she had made her knowledge available to her children through fairy stories – particularly *Grimm's Fairy Tales*, which Jane read voraciously, and the Bible.

As a Jewish girl the Star of David was familiar and through Bible reading the miraculous Christ child was known to her. However a golden child is uncommon in fairy tales. It may be that she had known one, but it has only come my way through searching *Grimm's Fairy Tales* to find 'The Golden Children'. Further afield the Hiranyagarbha of Eastern philosophy was translated by Muller as the 'Golden Child'; Hume and Zimmer rendered it as the 'Golden Germ'. Other analogies not accessible to Jane accrue from studying 'The Psychology of the Child Archetype', where Jung records the myths of little metal men and notes that the child is represented as the 'golden-ball'. All this group of images refer to the self and help in understanding the golden child as a narcissistic self representation. Further analogies could be pursued in alchemy which related gold to the lion, to the sun, and to faeces, thus rather directly expressing the infantile feeling that faeces are a precious part of the self and the equation of faeces with babies and birth (dropping down), which Jane and her brother had explicitly worked through together early on in their lives.

The self representations

It has been suggested that the golden child is a self representation – a self-symbol in the true sense that it unites opposites. This should not lead to overlooking that the whole dream is itself a self representation. This can be made clearer by applying the integrative–deintegrative model. Many years back Jung constructed the model of a typical dream.

He divided it up into the situation, the exposition, the development (peripetie) and the solution. Dividing Jane's dream up in this way results in the following:

1. *The situation*: 'I had a golden baby with a silver star on his forehead. One day I was standing by a river . . .'

2. *The exposition*: ' . . . and then an awful thing happened. My baby fell into the river.'

3. *The peripetie*: for the purpose of convenience this may be sub-divided into two parts: (a) 'Then I asked the dragon where she was and he said: "I'm going to keep her." (b) Then I stood on a triangle island with trees round about, I had a friend with me. Then some black children came and held hands surrounding the island. Then I said to my friend: "Let's push through the black children" – there was a gap between a few of the black children. We slipped through.'

4. *The solution*: 'I went to the river. I dived down and got my baby.'

This sequence, which will be studied in detail later on, can be abstracted as follows:

(a) It starts with an integrate: the 'situation'.
(b) Then there is a development which involves dividing up (deintegration) of the integrate in the 'exposition' and 'development'.
(c) Finally a new integrate is expressed in the 'solution' of the dream.

However, the representation is incomplete as all self representations must be. Within the self are the ego, the shadow, the father (dragon) and mother (in the identification of the child herself (the ego) with the maternal archetype). In addition the dragon may also, like the golden child, represent opposites. He is not only the father but also the sinister aspect of the mother who robs her of her magic baby, and her own greedy infant possessiveness as well. If so, 'he' represents a condensation which under other circumstances is differentiated into witches, queens, princesses and other representations.

As a postscript to these reflections it may be of interest to record that by the age of four years Jane was thinking in clear terms about herself, and she said on one occasion, 'I am a little bit of a baby, a little bit of a dolly and a lot of a mummy.' She would therefore have been in a position by nine years to understand the complexity of her inner world and its capacity to represent the primitive processes in her grief here idealised and largely worked through. If analysis had been needed, and it was not, Jane was the kind of child that could have understood her dream and its meaning. In spite of its beauty and the many analogies that could be developed much further than I have done, this dream is related to her life and her affects are expressed in imagery accessible to her understanding.

THE 'TRANSITUS' FROM MOTHER TO FATHER

The following dreams, selected from a longer series, show a development which occurred at a critical period of Christopher's life. He was a lively, sensitive boy aged five, referred because he wet the bed, suffered from 'gastric attacks' and offended his parents by expressing uncomplimentary opinions about others in their presence.

Dream 1

'My Dad smelt a smell of burning and we went in and there was a small flame that came from a match Dad had dropped. The flame danced like the fairies. My Mummy was very worried because the house might get burned, and you don't get anything back if the house is burned down.'

The central event in this dream is the fire seen by Christopher as a fairy flame. Fire as an object into which fantasy is projected is common amongst small children; not realising its objective properties, they may put their fingers into it, conceiving it as something to play with. Even when they do know its dangerous properties they continue to play with it and they may become excited by its heat and vitality, dancing or shouting when it flares up; Christopher sees it as dancing and so rhythmic. Rhythm can form the basis for a wide field of tranformative changes (c.f. Jung C.W.5, p.142 ff.).

The fairy world is related to nature in that fairies live in the earth, streams or woods, and represent a highly organised magical community of kings, queens, courtiers and so on. There are good and bad fairies who perform white and black magic. It is minor magic; they are neither as good nor as bad in their own right as are the major gods and devils. Of them an aetiological myth says:

> The popular belief in Ireland also is, that the fairies are a portion of the fallen angels, who, being less guilty than the rest, were not driven to hell, but were suffered to dwell on the earth. They are considered to be very uneasy respecting their condition after the final judgement. (Keightley 1982, p.363)

The collective significance of fire is further recorded in common speech; its universality as a symbol is revealed in the world-wide distribution of myths concerning its origin, and in innumerable others in which fire is a central feature. Fire can be understood to stand for the passion which this boy expresses in his behaviour and enuresis – there being a common association between dreams of fire and bed-wetting. That the fire is started by Christopher's father is of interest because he, like his son, is lively but erratic; thus the dream suggests an identification between the son and his father. By contrast Christopher's mother shows anxiety about a real possibility. As in the dream it is she in reality who keeps the rather unstable pair 'down to earth', thus providing a necessary compensation.

This dream portrays the individual responses of the child and his parents to what may figuratively be called the flame of life. That knowledge of the real parents can be easily used to further understanding suggests that Christopher has acquired a good appreciation of essential parts of their natures mainly through introjection.

Dream 2

'There was a witch who told me to make water in my mouth, and Mummy said, "no, not now". The witches chased Mummy and me and lots of other people. We sat on the rail outside the house. Witches chased witches – the ones [in front] got away by rolling over. The chasing witch slipped up and so the other one got away.'

'Making water in my mouth' refers to a way that Christopher used to bring saliva into his mouth by sucking in his cheeks. In Dream 1 the dynamic initiating object was fire; this time it is saliva, and its use suggests regression, since babies slobber over a spoon or other object, and later on spit with it to combine affection with abuse. 'Making water' also suggests urination.

Before the second dream but after the first Christopher had seen the film *Snow White and the Seven Dwarfs* which had made a considerable impression on him. Snow White is a virtuous princess, held captive and made to do the menial tasks of a servant by the evil queen her stepmother, who is a witch. From time to time the queen consults a magic mirror invoking a spirit of whom she repetitiously asks: 'Who is the fairest one of all?' As she invokes, flames rise up in the mirror; out of them the spirit appears and replies to her. The first time, the witch queen hears the reply she wants; it is she who is the most beautiful woman in the world, but the second time the spirit replies that it is not she but Snow White. At this, inflamed by envy, she seeks without success to kill Snow White, who flies into the woods, eventually to settle down with the dwarfs. Discovering where she has gone the queen, transforming herself by the aid of black magic into an old hag, sets out to find Snow White and induces her to eat the poisoned apple, whereupon Snow White falls into a trance from which she is eventually wakened by a prince, and thus virtue is rewarded and good triumphs over evil.

The conflict between good and evil runs through the whole story. In it the spirit of envy provides the starting-point for the subsequent drama. Christopher had been impressed by it and the idea of a witch started from it.

The picture of a red 'flaming' witch (c.f. Picture I) which Christopher painted is impressive, though very unlike a beautiful queen; she has virtually no trunk and a huge head on which the most prominent features are the eyes and a phallic hat; Christopher laid particular emphasis on the 'pointiness' of it. The absence of a body seems to deny its importance. If the picture is understood as the fantasy of a phallic mother, the penis-like hat suggests a displacement upwards of the genital organs. In view of his later Dream 5, the pointiness of the hat probably also refers, in a very concealed way, to his own erections. Emphasis on the eye also points to sexual interests, especially as the eye can

Picture 1 'The Witch'

represent the female genital, and anxieties about sexual differences in which he was in reality showing interest at this time.

The mythological association between the witch and the devil finds a parallel in his mother's history and indicates that Christopher has taken in (introjected) this part of her nature. In saying this there is no need to suppose that Christopher knew about his mother's childhood but rather that he felt inside him the emotional structures which his mother had developed as the result of her early life. Her father was a violent, brutal man, a 'devil' whom the mother feared in her childhood and whose influence had lasted to the present day. She is so bound to her childhood that even a small flame reminds her of the destructive experiences of bygone years; the negative content of her resistance to them is expressed in her restrictive conventional attitudes. By contrast Christopher's association was: 'Witches are always changing into something else.' Bearing in mind that his mother clings to the conventions, it is understandable that the witch who initiates change is a representation of her feared shadow: to become aware of this could mean returning to the 'hell' through which she passed in her childhood but also, unrealised by her, the potentiality for a change that she half-consciously expresses by coming for help over her child.

The witch is the appropriate form to embody the dark 'bad' side of the mother, because she compensates rigidity in being the expression of magical transforming powers, but she also links up with Christopher's belief in his own and his mother's omnipotence; the dream figure thus derives from the period of part object relations when the mother is good or bad and not both. The fairy story relates this characteristic to our cultural pattern and so helps to domesticate and give form to persisting ruthless trends. That the badness of a witch expresses a social form is shown by comparative studies. Witches are not always bad. Even though amongst primitive peoples they are held to be the cause of accidents, mistakes and personal and group catastrophes, yet the witch in our culture is a derivative of ancient fertility rites associated with the moon and the moon goddesses (c.f. Harding 1955). It has been in the course of history that the split between good and evil took a special place (c.f. Jung C.W.9 p.2), and so the witch became associated with the devil, her good counterpart being the Virgin.

Myths and fairy stories, and Snow White in particular, reflect the historical pattern and so become the container of persisting trends from early infancy; they enrich fantasy and dream in a form that is socially acceptable. Further to this it seems hardly worth saying that the child's anxiety fits in with the current social attitude that a bad (evil) person is to be avoided. So when the dream has 'lots of other people running away', and Snow White herself fled, this is a predictable response – it is really what lots of people do when confronted by evil; they try to escape, or, if they cannot do this, they 'sit on the fence'.

The dream continues: 'Witches chased witches'. It appears that where before there was the mother and Christopher and others, there are now *witches*. We know that fear can produce identification with the object of fear and this seems suggested by the dream which may be translated as saying, 'You become like a witch by running away; only when you detach yourself can you see what is happening.'

The way in which the one witch gets away from the other is significant: she 'rolls over' – an action which in reality would slow her down and make her easier to catch. Probably therefore this action is magical. Rolling over suggests a magic circle; through it nothing can penetrate, a theme that is amplified in the next dream.

Dream 3

'I was in a house, peeping out under the door. There was a "millman" who was coming across the river to burn the house down. He had come across the river. But there were soldiers, so it was all right. I think the "millman" was coming because we had taken something from his mill.'

The picture which the boy made (see Picture II) is of a mill with four sails, and round it is a circular river, thus combining a cross with a circle: a mandala-like structure, which Jung has defined as a symbol of the self and frequently associated with God. He says, for instance (C.W.11, p.56): 'The idea of those old philosophers was that God manifested himself first in the creation of the four elements. They were symbolised by the four partitions of a circle.' Again, ' . . . the quaternity is an age-old and presumably prehistoric symbol, always associated with the idea of a world-creating deity' (ibid., p.57). This amplification is not, I think, quite as fantastic as it may seem at first because Christopher had recently heard of God and was much preoccupied about him.

Picture II 'The Soldier, the Family House and the "Millman" '

If he had already connected the circle with magic and if god had seemed to him magical and threatening in defiance of current teaching the amplification begins to make sense, because Christopher would have made the necessary basic associations himself.

In dreams *belonging to* means being *equal to*, and so the mill is another aspect of the 'millman'. An amplifying of the generative meaning of the symbol occurs in Silberer's book (1917, pp.97–8) where he states:

> In symbolic language the mill signifies the female organ (*μυλλός*, from which comes *mulier*) and the satirist Petronius uses *molere mulierem* (grind a woman) for coitus, and Theocritus (Idyll, IV, 48) uses (*μύλλω*, I grind) in the same sense ... Like Apollo, Zeus, too, was a miller (*μυλεύς*, *Lykophron*, 435), hardly a miller by profession, but only in so far as he presides over the creative lifegiving principle of the propagation of creatures.

In the dream the 'millman' is threatening, because of a theft whose nature is not known, but the idea that God could be vengeful is familiar in the story of the garden of Eden, which Christopher may very well have heard. A further hint is given in the statement that the millman is coming 'to burn the house down'; it amplifies the first dream where the fire started by Christopher's father was feared by his mother because 'the house might get burned down'. Thus the two dreams amplify each other and from this one it can be inferred that the danger is imagined to come from the father's archetypal form.

The dream ends with the assurance that the defensive soldiers are sufficiently reliable.

Dream 4

'There was a witch and I loved her. So the witch put some poison on a rag and sprinkled it about and said: "You put your foot in this poison stuff." I said: "No thanks, I would rather have my mummy." So the witch said: "If you won't do this, I shall give you a poisoned apple." '

Christopher reflected and told me: 'I would not eat the apple – that would be a good trick, wouldn't it?' But he did not think of this in the dream.

The same night he also dreamed:

'I looked through a window into a room and my mum was talking to a witch and I said: "Is that your room?" and the witch shouted "Yes!" '

In this dream there is an obvious change in that both mother and child have developed a positive relation to the witch – the one by loving her, the other by conversation. When Christopher is with the witch his mother is in the background of his thoughts and is used as a retreat if the witch becomes too insistent, implying that his mother is the more omnipotent of the two. The change was clearly related to developments in the child's therapeutic situation for when he came to me his mother went to see a psychiatric social worker in another room. The danger from the witch is still present and related to his anal (the poison stuff) and oral anxieties (the apple). There is a link here with Snow White, for in that story it is the poisoned apple that sent Snow White to sleep.

Dream 5

'I went to the place we went to for a holiday but it was somehow different and I met Eunice and we went down a lane and there was a branch and I picked it up and there was a thing like a grass snake, you know a poisonous one. It stuck up . . . I jumped over it.'

In this dream his parents are absent. Eunice, Christopher's father stated, was 'a colourless girl', passive and receptive, thoroughly female and not unlike Snow White in the film.

That her personality makes her attractive is suggested by the grass snake that stands up like a penis.

Christopher fears the snake for it is poisonous – a reference to its bite and so once again to his oral anxieties. In addition it probably relates to his castration anxieties, for his mother has told him that if he touches his penis he will be taken to hospital where the doctors will cut it off, whilst his sexual interests have been sidestepped by her telling him to ask me for the answers to his questions.

So far the dream series as a whole reveals an increasing detachment of the child from his mother. In the course of it there are criticisms of her: she is afraid of the fire, of the witches, thus diminishing Christopher's belief in her omnipotence.

His mother's fallibility makes Christopher rely more on himself, yet it is not until his mother faces her shadow, the witch, that a new and feminine relationship can develop externally with Eunice; internally this means with a less omnipotent aspect of his anima. The development illustrates the thesis that a child tends to be fascinated and involved with the shadow of his parents whilst they have unsolved conflicts, and that when they take steps to solve them it is easier for him to free himself from them.

There is one more dream which came some months later:

Dream 6

'Gnomes digging in the ground. Daddy and I digging too. We found all kinds of things, all kinds of animals, cats, dogs, donkeys and tortoises. Put them in boxes and put them in a lorry and took them home. Then I had them.'

Father and son are digging with the gnomes. These are earth spirits, allied to the dwarfs who featured helpfully in the Snow White film; they are active, industrious spirits who, if properly treated, are helpful, though if their rules are not kept they revenge themselves speedily and in uncompromising fashion. They have magical powers of transformation and they guard the treasures of the earth, such as diamonds or other valuable material possessions.

The dream imagery follows up the earlier 'generative' amplification and also suggests a theme from the Bible in which Christopher had been showing interest, so possibly he had heard of it. 'And God said "Let the earth bring forth the living creature after his kind, cattle and creeping thing;

and beast of the earth after his kind; and it was so' (Genesis I, 25).

There are many aspects of these dramas which have not been elaborated. The amplifications on the 'millman' dream imply fantasies about the sexual relationship between his parents (the primary source) which occur during this period in maturation as part of the oedipal situation. From this it could be deduced that father and Christopher digging in the earth represented a fantasy of sexual potency arrived at by identification with his father in sexual intercourse with mother (the earth) thus magically implementing his wish for babies from his mother. Such inferences, however, would lead the discussion away from the primary aim of illustrating how a child uses myth and fairy story as a kind of food to enrich his dream life.

CONCLUSION

Christopher, his mother said, had been much impressed by the film *Snow White* when he went to see it. This means that he puts parts of himself (i.e. projected himself) into it and probably also identified himself with Snow White. Concurrently he took in the imagery, i.e. some introjection occurred, especially those parts of the film which can be traced in his dreams. The introjection is selective and comprises only those parts of the imagery that the child can use and assimilate. It is here that the active archetypes in the unconscious are assumed to come into operation, helping the ego in producing 'original' combinations relevant to this stage of maturation and his reaction to his parents. But more than this, the story or myth also facilitates his capacity to ally himself with collective and socially acceptable forms of inner and outer adaptation.

Though the origin of archetypal *imagery* in dreams is sometimes obscure this is usually due to technical difficulties. Sometimes the 'original' combinations correspond to those found in religion and mysticism of which the child has no knowledge. Study of these often clearly shows that the images and themes are built up in the course of the child's maturation by interaction between him and his environment. That children can actively construct archetypal images is certain and that they understand them in their own way is also beyond doubt. That they interpret them in the sophisticated ways developed by scholars, story-tellers and analysts is too patently absurd to be worthy of rebuttal.

It is, I hope, now clear that genetic factors and the maturing ego contribute to the formation of archetypal themes, but what impresses me most is the subtlety and inventiveness of a child's psychic processes. The understanding of which a child is capable is there to be fostered and guided by parents first and teachers second and this cultural heritage can thus become a living reality for a child whose sense of security and identity is thereby firmly established.

At the beginning of this chapter Jung was quoted as saying that some dreams in childhood shaped the child's 'whole destiny'. This conclusion derived from studies of striking dreams in childhood like the one recorded by Jacobi (1959) which seemed to foreshadow the eight-year-old child's death. It also derives from childhood dreams remembered by adults in analysis which sometimes give rather direct indications of the pattern of the patient's subsequent life. The dreams are often striking and it may be of interest to note that, as a grown woman, Jane remembered the dream of the golden child but not the other two I have cited. I do not unfortunately know what parts of it had become modified in her mind in the course of years nor how her subsequent development could be related to the dream.

That childhood dreams have long-term meaning, revealing clearly and dramatically significant patterns of life, is not in doubt. Like themes in play, like fantasies, and like memories also, they help to clarify critical periods in the formative years of individual development persisting and developing into mature characteristics of the adult.

4 Pictures

Jung's interest in pictures made by himself and his patients derived from their usefulness in giving non-verbal expression to symbolic images. He obtained them by using techniques of introversion aimed at releasing and raising unconscious fantasies to consciousness. He gave great importance to his picture 'method' as part of active imagination.

Since Jung thought the child was, as it were, immersed in the unconscious, I thought that, by adapting his techniques to child therapy, it would be possible to gain evidence for his thesis. It was this investigation that contributed forcibly to revising my ideas about the child's relation to the unconscious in its numinous aspect. It is perfectly true that from time to time fascinating symbolic forms are produced by children but as in dreams they are infrequent. Mostly children occupy themselves with depicting well-known objects: houses, trees, boats and ordinary people who are more common than ghosts, witches, magicians and archaic forms, even in the special setting of psychotherapeutic interviews. Myth-like symbolic figures can be found, though the older 'classical' ones are replaced by those derived from the now more exciting television serials.

The pictures discussed in this chapter, with the exception of the first scribbles, depict the more unusual kind of imagery. To get a wide perspective on children's ordinary pictures, their art and symbolic representations, this chapter must be supplemented by studying the other and larger volumes now readily available. Nevertheless those that follow represent common features of painting and scribbling in that they communicate, they symbolise, they give information about a child's psychopathology and reflect his inner feelings and events in his environment. All of them were obtained during diagnostic or therapeutic (not analytic) interviews when the child was under internal or external stress, and in this respect they differ from those made every day at home or in school. Sometimes their subject-matter was stimulated directly by me and in two out of four cases a dream was used to begin from – a technique recommended by Jung. The last series in an adolescent boy shows how he adopted a procedure closely akin to active imagination, as Jung describes it.

Case 1: Scribbling as a means of communication

Scribblings as a whole show extraordinary variety. Sometimes they are robust and strong, sometimes weak and trembling, sometimes they cover the whole page, sometimes no more than a tiny area. They have been studied in several ways but to ascertain their meaning the personal context of the scribbling is essential. For example, one small line on a piece of paper may be a statement that the child did not want to scribble, or it may actually be due to inhibition or even to physical illness.

The following scribblings (see Scribblings I, II, III, IV, V) were made by an attractive, intensely alive, sociable little girl, aged two and a half years, and were obtained as follows. She came upstairs and to my room with her brother, aged seven years, and was alarmed when I took her on my knee. But

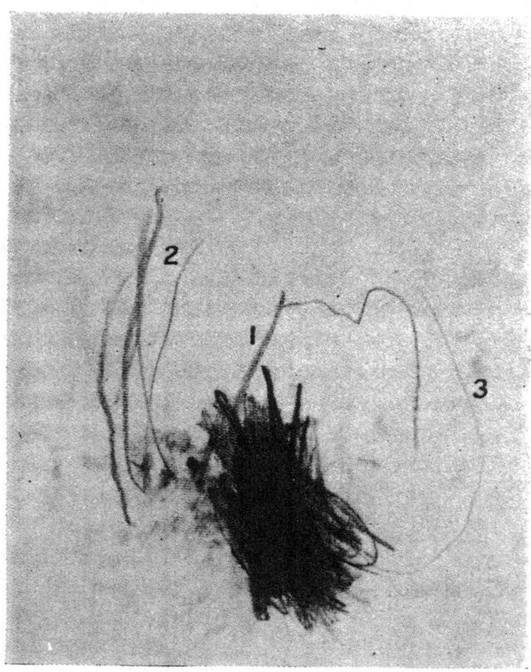

Scribbling I 'Protest'

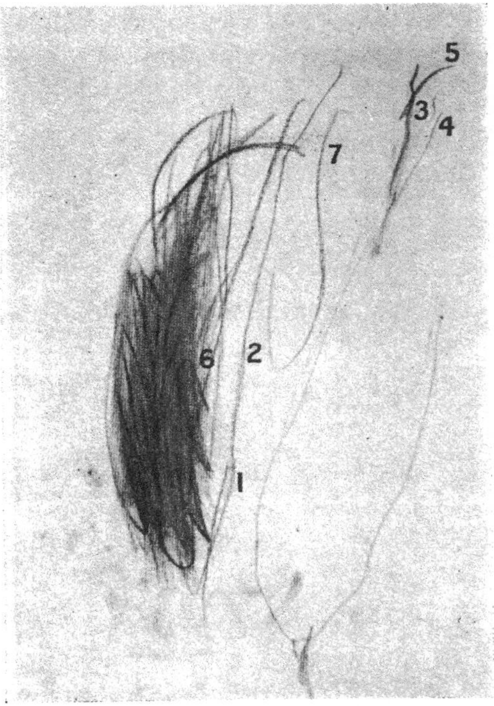

Scribbling II 'The Growth of Feeling'

when I gave her a piece of paper and some chalks she settled down to enjoy herself. Her brother was with us the whole time, and when I spoke to him about his sister, he confirmed or amplified what I said about her. Brother and sister seemed on easy terms; though she was said to dominate him, with me she did not take much notice of his existence.

The energy and vitality of her first complete scribble is at once striking. The effect of the picture corresponds to my impression of her as she drew, for each mark was made with firmness and precision. First she made a single line (1), then a group of them on the left (2), then a curved one (3), and finally she concentrated on the large black mark which focuses the picture. On this she expended much energy, shown by the numerous finger-marks made in the effort to hold the paper in position during her energetic rubbing.

She had used two sorts of line, soft and curved and

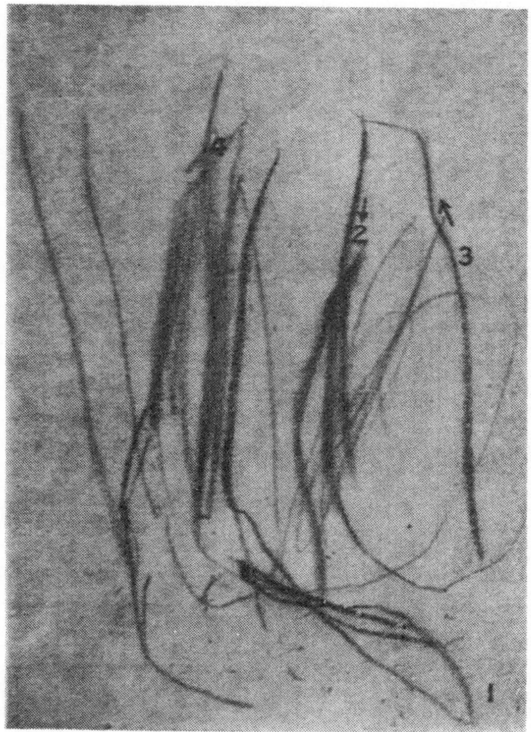

Scribbling III 'Diminution of Energy'

straighter ones. These were introductory and seemed to express the child's acceptance of what I had asked her to do. Then she became active and vigorous, and made the phallic and aggressive black mark. I understood this at the time to express her protest at being picked up.

The little girl used many colours but concentrated on black, perhaps the most sinister colour to children because of its association with darkness, and night fears of burglars, ghosts, bogeys, that can seem to invade the bedroom. The black mark, therefore, probably represents a bad object, perhaps my penis, close to where she sat, and her fears connected with it.

The little girl was plainly less anxious after her scribbling had been completed, as if she had decided I was not so dangerous as she had feared and had assimilated my, in reality, friendly approach. This conclusion is supported by the next picture, which contains the same elements, the phallic mark now being coloured.

The third scribbling shows less vigour; the lines are equally firm but there is more curve and less concentrated energy; the darker colour of the paper was her own choice. She seemed now to have exhausted her protest.

The fourth scribbling again shows the phallic mark, but the curves are even more pronounced than in the others, and the child has used light blue to make circular lines which occur above, to the right of, and below the red phallic mark. The picture seems more balanced than the previous ones, it is built up into an approximately oblong shape, the circles are above and below the phallic mark and loops are on the right.

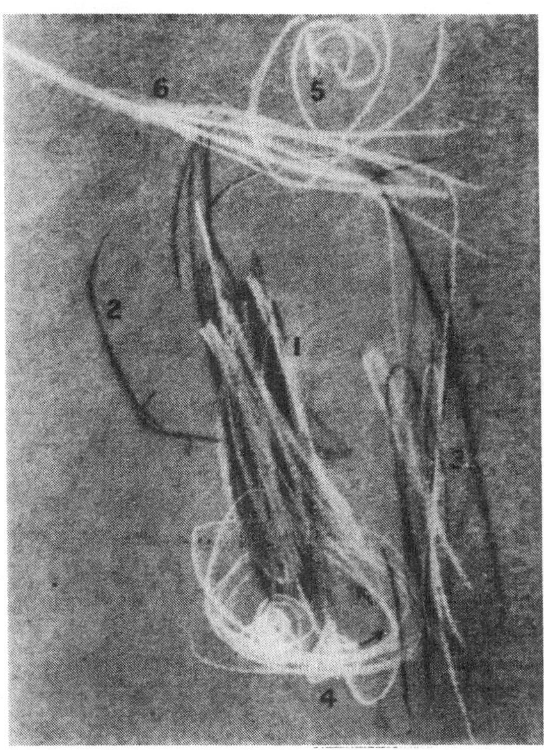

Scribbling IV 'Rhythm and Form'

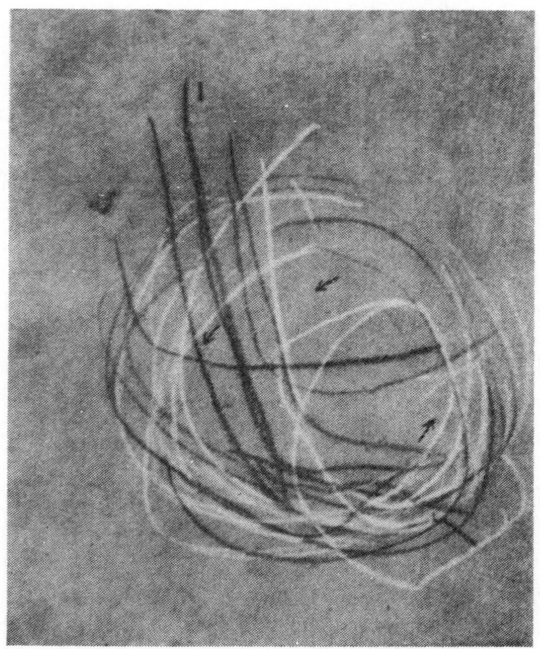

Scribbling V 'The Solution'

It covers the paper much more fully than the earlier scribbles and the whole begins to look more like a picture.

The final scribbling (V) is predominantly composed of rhythmical circular anti-clockwise movements and a few at first straight followed by curved yellow strokes. I have elsewhere (Fordham 1957) suggested that circular scribbles and pictures represent protective magic, completeness, and so represent a self-integrate. Applying this idea it might have been predicted that she would feel safe to depart; indeed she now got off my knee on to the ground and went about her own affairs.

This child, as shown by the richness and originality of her expression, was undoubtedly talented, but was probably going through difficulties in establishing herself as female on account of anxieties likely to be about sexual differences, especially if the phallic mark represented my penis.

Case 2: A picture used for diagnostic purposes

Henry, aged eleven, was brought to see me because he had been charged in court for stealing and running away from home. He was nervous, pale and on the verge of tears when I first saw him, and it was difficult to establish a relationship with him or to get information because he seemed 'deaf' (a symptom noted at school, where a medical examination had revealed no physical cause for it). He settled down to drawing using the paper, paints and pencil available on my table and I left him alone till he had finished (see Picture III). Then I asked him some questions about it but he could not bring himself to say much and soon became very nervous, and wanted to go to the lavatory. However, he told me that the big figures above the ship were the king and queen, the queen being in front of the king; he himself was keeping goal on the right of the picture. Little more emerged but after going hesitantly out of the room at the end of his interview he suddenly became indecisive, starting down the stairs, then he began to return, only to rush off as fast as he could.

The drawing consists of two apparently inconsequent parts: the two ships and the imposing 'king and queen' on the one hand, and the diminutive football match on the other in which the child himself is in a defensive position, perhaps indicating something of his relationship to other boys. The main body of the picture, in any case, lies behind him.

The 'king and queen' can be distinguished only with difficulty. Together they seem to form a single, strong, overpowering, even monstrous-looking figure. The crown is moon-like and carries a cross, the face is strong and the eye particularly gives an impression of latent power. The question-mark which appears in the place of an ear probably relates to the boy's deafness. The robes of the royal images have spikes down the back and front, like those on reptiles, the arms are embryonic, and the four feet, though evidently meant to represent those of two people, give the impression of belonging to a single creature.

A glance suggests the symbolical, quasi-mythological nature of the figures. The boy said that only the queen can be seen, and he has drawn her in the sky with the moon as her crown. It seems to represent a fantasy of a moon mother who passes through the sky as the moon does. These reflections lead

Picture III 'The King and the Queen'

easily into mythology in which the moon is ambivalent: it brings fertility and is the cause of insanity (lunacy).

Though the figure is meant to be a queen she has, however, male characteristics as well, suggested by the rough brutish appearance suggesting that a combination has taken place and a confusion of sexual characteristics has resulted. The unity of male and female is, however, an archetypal idea. Jung has worked on it and published his conclusions in several books, but especially *Mysterium Coniunctionis* (C.W.14), to which reference may be made.

Turning to the ship, which is below the figure, it has unusual characteristics: the anchor is much too big and hangs at an unnatural angle; the king's head, which might well be expected to breast the waves, is located at the stern, and the smoke and flag blow in opposite directions. The captain's position at the wheel makes it impossible for him to see what is in front because the superstructure of the ship interferes between himself and his line of vision.

The contradictory behaviour of the flag and smoke suggests that two winds are being imagined, blowing in opposite directions, and this correlates with his state of indecision (ambivalence) when he left the room.

The picture indicates the invasion of archetypal fantasy, not altogether unusual in a boy of eleven. But it gives a pathological impression, and this, along with his symptoms, reveals the weakness of his ego which seems to be independent of the archetypal forms. It is as if he felt on the defensive in an impersonal and frightening world.

Turning therefore to consider what had produced this state of affairs, it might have been that this child was himself psychotic, but he did not give that impression. Moreover his family life had broken down because Henry's mother had recently died. This in itself must have been traumatic, and makes it likely that the mother in the sky (in heaven) relates to his feelings about her. In addition his father was showing signs of schizophrenia, and his delusions seem to relate to Henry's picture.

One night Henry's father put a milk bottle outside the front door and looking out of the window he saw a light shining on it. At first he thought this came from the moon but, as the bottle was in the shadow, this conjecture could not be true; so he looked more carefully and was surprised to find that the moonlight was reflected from opera-glasses focused on his house. This he concluded was proof of malicious intent: somebody was spying on him. His paranoid delusion was ineffective and may relate to the ineffectual arms of the figure in the picture. Further, the dominance of the mother figure in the picture is analogous to the father's history. In his early life he had been dominated by his mother, and he only married late in life to a motherly woman who contained him as his mother had done before. By now it may be suspected that the boy's picture contains a fantasy about his father's psychic state, and there are more analogies which support this idea. For instance, the father could not understand why he was spied upon, but in his delusion he was forced to build defences based on a misinterpretation of reality. The result is not unlike the captain who is placed so that the superstructure of the ship intervenes between the steering wheel and the view of the ocean ahead.

Inasmuch as the son is able to express his father's pathology in an oblique way he seems to have introjected his psychoses. The subsequent identification may also be inferred through the small boat which trails behind the steamer.

To use the boy's picture as I have done is, in my opinion, useful, even though it seems to lead away from Henry's tragic personal situation.

Case 3: The ghost and the child

The next picture made by a six-year-old boy, James, was derived from the following dream: 'I am lying in bed, a ghost comes out of the cupboard, comes into my bed and swallows me.' I suggested that he make a picture and the result was Picture IV. After he had made it I learnt that he had a generalised fear of ghosts.

His dream dramatically illustrates the process of introjective identification, and so suggests a very early origin for his fear. In early dreams of children, swallowing and biting are important (c.f. supra pp.31ff.). But the picture also contains more complex fantasies and techniques of expressing himself, since fantasies and dreams of ghosts themselves occur, later than the earlier ones of being attacked and sometimes eaten by animals.

James's relation to his mother was difficult. She loved him but had a violent temper and maltreated him in consequence. She wanted to get help because of her guilt about her behaviour. It is of interest that at this time she dreamed that

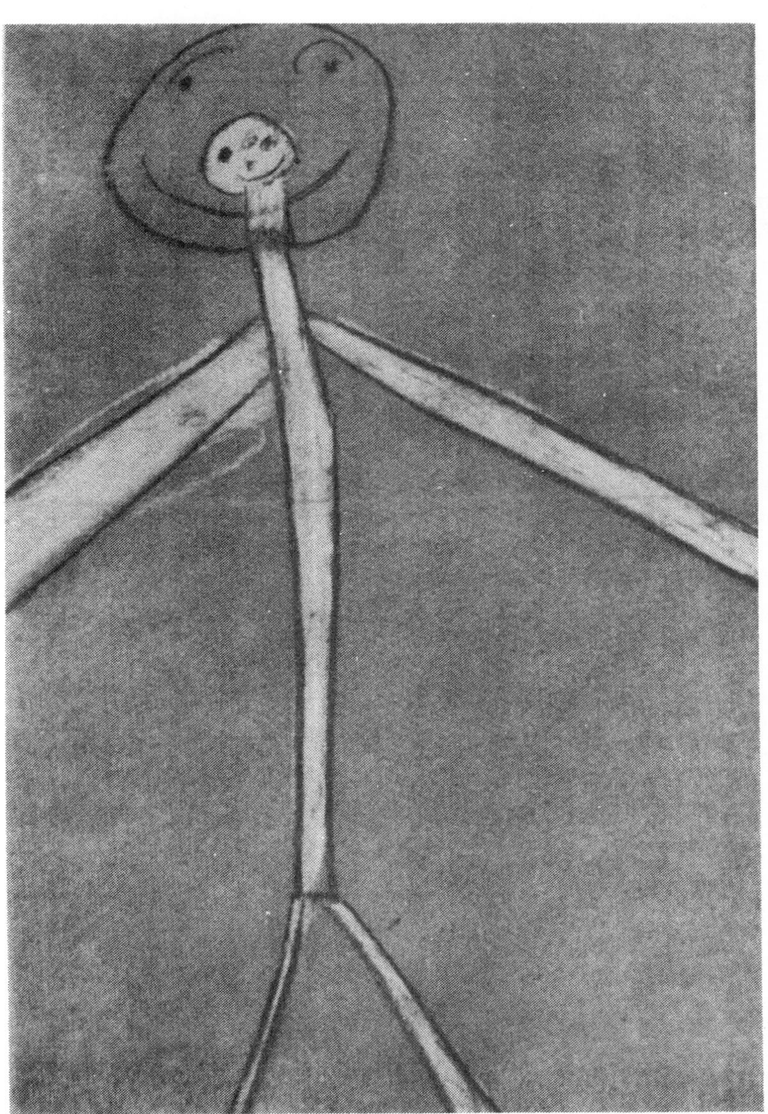

Picture IV 'The Ghost and the Child'

her dead psychotic father rose from his grave as a ghost. Whether dreams were talked about at home is not known, nor was it possible to define how far the child's dream was contributed to by identification with his mother. However, at this time she was trying to give more freedom to her son, whom she had previously kept under close surveillance because of his frequently violent and sometimes uncontrolled behaviour.

In his play with me, James could indeed become exceedingly violent, and he would throw stones at me hard enough for it to become necessary to take at least some defensive action. I pointed out the danger, told him that I would not let him treat me in this way, and that I meant it. As words proved ineffective I pretended to counter-attack and he then ran away. In this fashion a game would result, leading to his becoming sexually excited, so there was evidence of homosexual trends in his make-up.

One day he painted my face and neck a dark brownish red. I suspected that this might be connected with his fears and raised my arms to the position of the ghost in the picture, little guessing, however, the fear I should arouse in him; he crouched terrified in the corner of the room and shouted to me to stop.

An analogy with initiation rituals

There are a number of features of primitive initiations which are strikingly like the child's fantasies and my behaviour. The following details are drawn from Layard's study of the tribes of Malekula:

1. Initiation into manhood is begun at any age between four and twenty-two.

2. The aim of the initiation is eventually to remove the child from the influence of his mother and initiate him into the corporate body of men in the tribe.

3. During the first five days of the novices' confinement in the initiation house, no moment is free from the fear that some hoax or other may be played on them ... their general tone is ... based on terrorising the novices and, in particular, frightening them with the alleged homosexual appetites of ghosts.

> 4. A recurring theme is for the initiates to divide themselves into two parties, one outside the house and one within. Those inside, including the tutors, dance and sing songs ... lulling the suspicions of the weary novices by every means in their power when, suddenly, in burst the others, disguised with paint to represent the ghosts of old men (*ta-mat mot*). Sometimes matters are so arranged that the tutors win, and the ghosts will break through and strike a novice, to his dismay. (Layard 1942)

This parallel is of interest (and particularly so to me) because it seemed that I had unwittingly adopted something like a method of 'hoaxing' and terrifying James, and that I had also roused homosexual feelings in him. Further, the aim of the treatment had been to work for greater independence for him, and this meant allowing a transference to develop through which his anxieties could be lessened and he could establish the identification with his own father, and that had not occurred.

The analogy thus gives interesting insight into what may be called the initiatory aspect of the kind of play therapy I was using and also into the nature of the anxieties which are evoked and worked through in such procedures.

Case 4: Symbolic transformation

John was a large, rather uncouth boy, aged fourteen years, who hid his anxiety under a cloak of common sense and the defensive statement that everything was 'all right'. In reality he was threatened with expulsion from school where, in spite of a good intelligence, his work was bad and he was considered an unsatisfactory pupil in ways that were not clearly stated. In his treatment it soon became evident that he was offering passive resistance to those in authority.

His fear and helplessness were revealed in the following dream which, he said, repeated itself with minor variations again and again.

'I go with some friends for a picnic in a field and as we are sitting there a bull charges at us. We all run away but the bull makes a special attack on me, he seems to choose me out from the others. I try to hide behind a tree but the bull knocks the tree down and I wake up. Once I was actually tossed by the bull.'

Drawing II (copy of the original)

This dream became the starting-point for a series of drawings (Drawing II). The boy was quite easy to get on with so long as his school problem was left alone, and when he became more accustomed to the therapeutic situation he began to scribble on the blackboard.

The images he drew were made in the following order. First there was the ship which he had seen downstairs in a picture that hung in the hall of the clinic. Underneath he sketched in outline a sea monster snorting through its nostrils. Next he drew the bull, himself, and the tree in a field. The face in the tree was put in after I pointed out that one seemed to be there though he had not intended it. Then he made the image clear and told me that in his dream the tree actually jeered at him, tried to trip him up with its roots as he ran from the bull, and that though he prayed to the tree to help him it was no use. It seemed to him that the tree-spirit and the bull were allied against him, and this he showed by drawing a line joining them together. That he felt isolated between them is expressed by a line encircling himself.

The aeroplane, he said, attacks the ship 'just as the bull attacks me', and he drew a straight line to represent aggression, and added a curved one to represent the association between bull and aeroplane.

He next turned back to his dreams to find a subject for further drawing. Some of those that followed were made rapidly and spontaneously as if he did not know how they were going to turn out. Others were made deliberately in the sense that he knew what he meant to draw; again additions were put in as the result of reflection or as reactions to my remarks. Thus the result grew up through interaction between his ego and the more spontaneous fantasies, just as happens in active imagination.

The series of pictures on the left was begun deliberately. Figure 1 is a drawing of the tree-spirit, but the heads that follow grew of themselves. After they had been completed he gave two of them names: the one on the left he called the 'devil' and No.5 on the right was the 'Chinaman'; 2 and 3 had no names, but their hats and configuration make it clear that they are variants of the Chinaman. Animal, tree-spirit, devil and Chinaman were closely related to each other by association.

The elements in these drawings may be compared with religious symbolism. The association of the devil with the bull, for instance: the former was indeed partly derived from

Dionysos and the cults or the devil included comparable orgies. The 'animal' elements represented in the pagan religions are also found in Christianity as the lamb of God or the four evangelists, but trends in Christianity in favour of asceticism were too strong, so symbols used in pagan religions suggest themselves.

The conflict situations of adolescence stem from feeling sexual changes in the body which cannot have adequate outlet, partly at least because of inhibitions imposed by the culture pattern. Drives are developing which need to be integrated if the adolescent is to play his part in the world, yet society demands abstinence and consequently regressive trends can assert themselves, especially if oedipal conflicts have not been lived through and resolved by holding identifications. The sexual conflicts of adolescence, therefore, may be roughly defined by the need to discover how sexuality can be controlled without its becoming 'the devil'.

Figure 4 in the series of pictures is the 'devil', Figure 5 is a 'Chinaman'. The devil is connected with the doing of something evil, but the Chinaman is different. This boy produced his pictures in 1938 when the Chinese were still thought of as mysterious members of secret societies. Figure 5 was more spontaneous than Figure 4, whose drawing is clear and definite: each line is complete, in contrast to the jerks and breaks in the drawing of the devil.

Nevertheless his devil was felt by John to be real and dangerous, for his next painting, a 'totem devil', was made to 'scare devils away'. It was also, he said, 'something inside which diamonds can be put for safety'.

This striking symbolic picture (see cover) is dominated by an ingenious combination of three faces, two looking in opposite directions. The third is looking forward and has characteristics of the Chinaman but its main feature is a huge mouth. The boy was as surprised by the result as I was; the picture evolved rapidly and spontaneously, indeed it only took him about ten minutes to paint. It was built up as follows: he began by making quite a simple phallic figure with an oblong on top (painted over and so not visible in the end product), then he added a star, then a diamond, and below this a square. The pattern as a whole was next outlined in black and the diamond and square shapes inside received yellow outlines filled in with blue.

The boy evidently wanted to express his feelings of real

evil power by black, but there is also, particularly in its lower trunk, much colour, which makes it very positive. John drew the lower phallic part first and on top of this he put the black part. At first the demons were absent; only as the conception developed did the idea of devils creep in.

Once again, as in Case 3, the anxieties of infancy are elaborated into a sophisticated picture. The mouth is symbolised and structured in a way of which a small child would be incapable. It suggests fierce teeth held apart and organised into a magic-like circle. It may be that here is another facet of John's passivity based on cruel feelings about biting (oral sadism) originating in infancy. The two, it seems, have become welded into a symbolic image of awe-inspiring and numinous intensity. To refer to its infantile roots seems almost insulting and so it would be if the achievement of reaching them and the defences against them were not so effectively organised. Here in short is the answer to those who might want to depreciate his defences and ignore the ongoing element that they represent when combined into a living symbol, the heir of a transitional object.

5 THE CONCEPTUAL MODEL

The conceptual framework used in this book is based on three theoretical entities: the ego, the archetypes and the self.

THE EGO

Jung defined the ego as the centre of consciousness in most of his work, though he recognised the existence of unconscious parts of it in the shadow. This compact formulation can be expanded as follows: the ego is the sum of perceptual acts and motor discharges that are or can become conscious.

Just when consciousness of any kind begins can only be inferred, because the study of intra-uterine life is manifestly difficult, but, enough is now known about the foetus to state confidently that he experiences some kind of rudimentary consciousness. Rapid as development may be after birth, the ego can play only a small part in the infant's existence, which is best understood in terms of patterned archetypal drives. Soon, however, ego fragments can be noted; they are closely related from the beginning to the unconscious fantasy representations. As the ego becomes stronger it deploys methods of organising and controlling mental life and defences begin to form. Since many of these cannot be consciously controlled the identification of the ego with accessible states of consciousness becomes dubious.

However, the ego concept is extended to include parts of the psyche which are not and cannot easily achieve consciousness, and it becomes necessary to define the attributes to be ascribed to it. The following list gives characteristics which a relatively mature ego may display, together with amplificatory notes on each as it seems necessary.

1. Perception

Consciousness is based on perception but not all afferent stimuli in the nervous system are perceived, and further not all perceptions reach the threshold of consciousness.

2. Memory

Undoubtedly remembering is an essential element in mental functioning, but memories of past events in the life of an individual are to be treated with caution since, though some events may be recorded realistically, others are complex structures which change over time whilst in either case their emotional importance and meaning can alter significantly.

3. Organisation of mental contents

Jung defined thinking, feeling (valuing), sensation and intuition as the functions of consciousness; introversion and extraversion are its two attitudes which may alternate. These functions and attitudes may be unconscious or conscious. In addition the ego contributes to fantasy formation though the archetypes also influence a large part of it and exerts the decisive effect on its development.

4. Control over mobility

This means control over impulsive acts as well as ordinary movements.

5. Reality testing

6. Speech

7. Defences

Under this heading are included a number of strategies which result from conflict situations giving rise to anxiety. Some defences which predominate in infancy are rooted in very primitive states of the self. They are projective, introjective, identification and idealisation. Others develop as the ego gains strength and particular types of individual use some more than others. The following is a list of these defences: isolation, reaction formation, undoing, rationalisation (particularly evident in obsessional personalities), conversion, repression, dramatisation and acting out (to be observed best in hysterical reactions); displacement which is too widespread to associate with any particular group of personality organisation.

At first these defences were understood negatively as structures that under optimal conditions could be dispensed with. But when it was gradually recognised that they could not be eliminated, the door was open to understanding them as part of the ongoing process of maturation. Since this never ends and since, in developing specialised functions and attitudes, only parts and some forms of psychic activity were useful, they were recognised as inevitable and desirable so long as they remained plastic. Only when they became unadapted, inappropriate and rigid did they take on the wholly negative characteristics first attributed to them.

8. Capacity to relinquish the ego's controlling and organising functions

Jung gave much attention to this capacity as an essential feature in his study of individuation, where he lays stress on the need for the conscious ego to recognise other powers within the psyche, represented in the archetypal forms, and also its subservience to the self. However, this is a capacity which is also needed at other periods of life, and particularly in childhood though in early infancy the ego is not sufficiently established to warrant it being said that it gives up something which it has not yet achieved.

It will be noticed that some characteristics of the ego are clearly related to archetypal processes and structures and this applies to most of perception, fantasy, mobility and defence, indeed the existence of perceptual data, whether derived from the environment or from the archetypes, presupposes ego functions in existence. I mention this because, though some psychic structures and functions can become relatively autonomous, a strong and healthy ego is related to the foundations of the personality as well as to reality.

THE ARCHETYPES

Though most studied in their complex symbolic forms, i.e. in dreams, fantasies, mythology, folklore and religion, the essential core that emerges from Jung's work is that an archetype is a psychosomatic entity having two aspects: the one is linked closely with physical organs, the other with unconscious psychic structures. The physical component is the source of libidinal and aggressive 'drives'; the psychic one is the origin of those fantasy forms through which the archetype reaches incomplete representation in consciousness. Whereas the organism is object-seeking and capable of relatively few though developing applications, fantasy can expand in many ways, use various objects, and sometimes, especially in pathological cases, display relatively unlimited variety.

It may be of interest to mention here that a number of concepts, having a similar aim to that of the archetypes, have been introduced into child psychology by the members of other schools of thought: Spitz has used the idea of organisers in his study of infants during the first year of extra-uterine life, whilst the concept of unconscious fantasy operating in the child from birth has been developed by Kleinian psychoanalysts; Piaget may also be mentioned in that he made use of a theory of innate schemata in his studies. All these have followed similar lines of thought to those introduced by Jung as early as 1919 when he used the term 'archetype' for the first time.

Without attempting to compare these views, they all meet the need for a theory of structures to account for behaviour very early on in the infant's life. The archetype concept, as it is developed here, is one amongst these.

The imagery through which archetypes express themselves is varied. In infancy it is often, but not always, different from that met in childhood, adolescence and middle age, the latter period being the one from which Jung drew most of his clinical data and on which he based his theory. This led me to realise the importance of his distinction between the archetype as a theoretical entity and the empirical imagery and behaviour which the concept organises. The archetypes in infancy, i.e. during the first two years of life, are not nearly so differentiated as they become later on, because, at any rate to begin with, behaviour and imagery cannot be detached the one from the other: the imagery is bodily. In spite of these differences, the patterns of behaviour are related to unconscious archetypal forms and can be traced in developmental sequences and so link on to the complex symbolic imagery of later life.

THE SELF

Introducing the concept of the self into child psychology has needed something of a revolution in the thinking of analytical psychologists because the concept, as developed by Jung, was most applied to religion and to the later part of the life of individuals. It is not easy to begin thinking about the roots of these processes in childhood, let alone infancy, without some sense of shock or outrage. Such at least was my experience when I discovered symbols of the self in the dreams and fantasies of small children. This happened during World War Two and it was not till the channels of communication with Jung were re-established that I discovered that he himself had come to the same conclusion from his study of children's dreams.

These data needed evaluation. What purpose did the experiences serve? It was clear that they were related to the child's self-feeling, his sense of self-esteem and of identity, all feelings which could attain consciousness and so must be linked to the ego. This led on to the idea of there being some particular dynamic relation between the ego and the self.

At the time my ideas were starting to develop there was a strong trend amongst analytical psychologists to conceive of the self as a stabilising, centralising and even closed system, though Jung's later work often suggests the opposite. My interest in children, however, gave rise to doubts about conceiving the self in this way. However relevant the emphasis on stability and organisation may be in other contexts, it is not suitable when applied to the changing and developing period which infancy and early childhood represent. The idea of the self as an integrator alone leaves no room for the emergence of part systems brought into being by the dynamic patterned drives and environmental stimuli. This, then, was an important motive for introducing a more dynamic model and led to the idea that the self might be a more unstable system than had so far been conceived.

The next question to ask was: could it be that the system which the self representations indicated is primary, and further, could it be that the infant or foetus might be looked on as a unity, the self, from which the archetypes and the ego derived? This would appear to fit in with Jung's idea that the self was the organism as a whole, of which the ego and the archetypes and the body were aspects.

When these ideas were developing, it was becoming apparent that the dynamic processes in early childhood were far more complicated than had previously been thought possible; so how could their apparently organised though rapidly changing nature be accounted for alongside a theory of the ego which was then supposed to develop a noticeable degree of organisation by four or five years of age? To be sure, the theory of archetypes would account for much of what was observed, but the degree of total organisation which an infant reveals needed to be taken into account as well.

Aim-directed behaviour, fantasies, thoughts, feelings, perceptions and impulses, all of which can be described separately in dynamic terms, do not grasp the child's nature as a whole unless it is realised that each group of experiences is linked to others not being activated at any particular time. Recognition of these interrelations does something towards expressing the organic wholeness and individuality of the child in which his sense of identity is founded.

Bearing in mind the theory current in analytical psychology some thirty years ago that the ego is a negligible entity up to what is, to a child analyst, a relatively mature age (about four years), it appeared inconceivable that a child before that age could be considered sufficiently organised to treat analytically. Yet many children between two and a half and three years were being successfully treated. Conceiving the self as a primary entity, the sum of part systems, and introducing the idea that they could deintegrate out of the self and then integrate again, might account for the possibility of treating a small child as a unit separate from his parents.

The idea of the self as expressed in steady states of integration alone is changed radically by this view, for it assumes that during maturation unstable states recur, sometimes involving part and sometimes the whole of the self. They last for a short or a long time, yet the whole self continues in being. The unstable states are not, in health, disintegrations, which mean splitting of the ego, they are rather changes in orientation which involve the whole person at first and later parts of it as maturation proceeds. The stabilising entity is at first the self only, but soon the ego contributes and ensures that the dynamic sequences in the self do not prove unproductive and circular, but are changed by ego activity which in turn increases its strength. Thus the structuring of the psyche is brought about to a significant extent by the ego. Without it only repetitive archetypal deintegrative reactions would exist, and these, though adaptive, would not lead to permanent interacting structures.

Since the time that the self concept was originated, much more has been discovered about ego fragments, and there can be no doubt that quite a firmly established ego structure is in being by two years of age; therefore the concept of the self may not be so necessary or central. The new data have indeed suggested an alternative theory of the ego, just because its organisation begins much earlier than was believed. It is indeed tempting to develop a new model altogether, in which the ego is made to include all psychological dynamisms. But it follows, if this model is to cover all the variety of data available, that the ego must be divided up into sub-systems so as to describe the different kinds of experience that can be made the subject of empirical study; otherwise the model must be still born. This dividing up of the ego was done by Fairbairn (1952), who distinguished a central, a libidinal and an antilibidinal ego. In this model the self ceases to be a primary datum and is made redundant except as an aspect of or even identical with the ego itself. The concept of unconscious archetypes must equally be treated as invalid, since they too are conceived as ego structures.

From analytical psychologists this model may not receive even the notice that it deserves – but it has elsewhere been given considerable attention and so needs to be recorded even if only to reject it.

The archetype theory explains primitive modes of behaviour and more than anything the existence of organised fantasies in a child and infant with minimal ego characteristics as defined above. It is these and the self that the analyst of small children relates to for much of the time rather than a coherent ego. It was perhaps the experience of analysing small children that, to my mind, favoured the self as a primary entity rather than the ego: it leaves room for data suggesting that the analyst acts as an auxiliary ego for the child rather than the controlling ego structures residing in the small child himself. As part of the working theory used here, then, the self will be treated as indispensable.

Since I first put forward my views, the postulate that the self is of central importance in maturation has been taken up by a number of analytical psychologists. Reflections about it are contained in Jacobi's book on individuation and she also published a small paper on this topic (1953). Neumann (1954) produced some ingenious speculative ideas, particularly about the relation of the ego and the self which he held are difficult to distinguish in childhood; he also introduced a concept of the ego–self axis which Edinger developed and related to clinical observations. Aldridge (1959), Hawkey (1945, 1951, 1955, 1964), Kalff (1962) and Tate (1958, 1961) all made valuable observations on clinical states in which self representations could be defined, and Kellogg's studies of children's finger paintings (1955) contain fascinating evidence of how mandala patterns are built up and lead to pictures of people. Self symbols were also found to be a uniting element in groups of children studied by Lewis (1953).

An important next step in my thinking was to develop the theory of the self in childhood by postulating that the infant is primarily a unit or self at the start. In this view I remained alone for some time till Enid Jacobson's researches which culminated in her book *The Self and the Object World* (1964–65). There she postulates a primary psychosomatic unity – the self – whose energy is neutral, neither libidinal nor aggressive. In her book she argues the advantages of this postulate over Freud's concept of primary narcissism, which developed into primary masochism when he introduced his dual drive theory.

Support for this concept was evinced by Jacobson when she used it in the analysis of psychotic patients. I myself have found it useful in many ways, amongst which I want to mention here the study of autistic children with minimal relation to the external world; indeed they seem to have developed no distinction between what is themselves and what another person or object. Forty of these children have been intensively investigated by Bettelheim; though he does not explicitly postulate a primary unity or self he clearly recognises the importance of sustaining a positive attitude towards the autism and provides conditions under which the child can himself emerge from it by a process cognisant with deintegration–integration processes.

Accepting then the primary psychosomatic unity of infants, the model which I began to formulate in 1947 has now been developed as follows: the primary or original self of the infant is radically disrupted by birth in which the psychosoma is flooded by stimuli both internal and external which give rise to prototypic anxiety. Following this, a steady state re-establishes itself and the first clear sequence of disturbance followed by resting or steady states has been completed. The sequence repeats again and again during maturation and the motive forces behind them are called deintegrative and integrative. At first the sequences are rapid, but as psychic organisation proceeds, they become spread over longer periods till relative stability is attained for most of the time. It is now possible to define a number of periods at which one or other or both of these processes can be studied: birth, the approach to mother centring round breast feeding, with particular references to changes occurring round about three months, seven months and weaning; the separation–individuation phase (c.f. infra p.99ff.); the crisis created by the birth of a sibling; and oedipal developments. Following this the stable latency period leads to the disturbances of adolescence and to a relatively stable maturity, which continues till the transition to later life when deintegration–integration sequences repeat and the individuation processes, which Jung specifically investigated, begin.

SELF REPRESENTATIONS

In the above discussion the self has been referred to in (a) theoretical terms and (b) as a system of representations, some of which must be classed as symbolic in Jung's sense.

What is a representation? This can be understood with reference to unconscious structures and especially the archetypes. They are not directly known because they are unconscious. They can, however, be partially known through a class of images called archetypal, which represents the unconscious archetype. Similarly the primal self cannot be represented but its deintegrates can, and from these inferences can be made about the self.

I now come to projective identification. I have found that there is sometimes a confusion about its relation to deintegration: I will attempt to clarify it because the two processes are not the same, though deintegration must have taken place and produced some psychic structure before projective identification can take place. In projective identification a part of the self enters into another self and identifies with a part of that other containing self. There it can destroy more or less of the containing self or it can provide information about it, which can be integrated when the projection is withdrawn. It can therefore be a primitive form of perception and, because the process can be experienced unconsciously by both parties, it is also a primitive form of communication especially when ego boundaries are weak as we assume is the case in an infant and its mother, when she regresses when caring for her baby. I consider that projective identification gives rise to states described as primitive identity, participation mystique and fusion.

I also assume that projective identification is a powerful method of forming archetypal images: indeed the process occurs in such mythological themes as the entry into the mother monster with the aim of destroying her from within, or the dual mother theme with her ideal and terrible characteristics. I called the underlying objects behind these archetypal images self-objects, to include the period before definable fantasy images are formed.

In studying these very primitive states it is important not to overlook the enormous amount of work that has gone into cognitive development during infancy and early childhood. In infant observation and childhood this can easily be done because the emphasis is on the infant's emotional life in relation to his mother. In these studies little emphasis is laid on the dichotomy conscious–unconscious; indeed there seems to be little place for these concepts which are so useful later on.

I hold that the uselessness of them is indicative of the fluid state of infant experience where there are such quick changes in interest and intention, and emotional changes between love and hate, that it seems a positive interference to start to think in those terms. Yet the infant does show evidence of structured behaviour. Certainly the witnessing of persecuted and depressive conditions, or his behaviour at the breast and other nuclear situations give evidence of mental and emotional structures at work. Therefore we cannot say that there is no ego though we have evidence that many of the structures are archetypal, resulting from deintegration. In bringing the infant into relation with his environmental mother, however, he gains experience which makes the formation of images inevitable. It seems also inevitable that these give rise to a form of consciousness which gradually integrates to form a more and more coherent ego. The building up of a definable distinction between consciousness and unconscious states does happen later, and Bion thinks of them as being due to the formation of a barrier of alpha elements (Bion 1970).

What are the characteristics of the symbols? Jung defined a fair number: the mandala, the child, the philosophic tree, images of divine beings and God in particular – they all have a totality or cosmic reference. Whilst symbols of this kind occur in childhood they are infrequent and much more study has been given to the way self feelings mature in the ego: they depend upon formation of the body image. The infant's cosmos is a self cosmos in the first place and is restricted to body images. He knows nothing of philosophic trees, God, mandalas, etc. Nevertheless his experiences are of an all-or-none, i.e. total, kind which come to be represented in omnipotent feelings of the following kind: he himself has the feeling of being the whole of his 'cosmos', comprising objects which have 'magical' power which he exerts, or of which his feeble ego is the victim. Here lie feelings that recurrently dominate the infant's life till the boundaries between himself and his external world become recognised. It is these feelings that the infant ego gradually represents in fantasies, in dreams, picture-making, in play and in verbal interchanges.

It seems clear that though at birth the infant is object-related, the nature of his objects is composite. There are some that are objective but the main bulk of perceptions are heavily loaded with energy from within the deintegrate of the self. This energy organises the perception so that the object becomes what may be termed a self-object. I will consider self-objects in more detail later.

As deintegration–reintegration sequences occur the results of their functioning become stable and as the body image is formed and with it a clearer perception of what is within it and what is outside it, there develops within the child a perception of himself and the outside world. Once established the infant distinguishes between what is self and not self – it has been a formidable achievement of the ego. He can now develop a whole range of feelings, images and thoughts about himself which may be grouped for convenience into what he would wish to be or what he fears he may become – i.e. a hero, a parent, a gangster, etc. All these are more or less related to the original totality as expressed in omnipotent feelings. Inasmuch as they do so they not only refer to the condition of the ego but also to the self.

As ego growth continues, the feelings, originally omnipotent, integrate into a sense of identity in a person continuously the same in space and time. When this has taken place self feeling can become more realistic and the infant can relate as a person to others in his environment and to the object world in a more and more extended sense. But inasmuch as the self feeling excludes earlier affective states or inasmuch as they are objectified and need to be so, the omnipotent or wishful feelings become related to the sophisticated symbolic expressions found particularly in religion. These feelings once developed and refined form an important aspect of the growing child's relation to society.

SOURCES OF DATA

One advantage of constructing an abstract model is that it can be used to give a very compressed account of data. In addition a position is reached from which thoughts can be manipulated so that further understanding of affective states is made possible. Under favourable circumstances new light is thus shed on areas of the psyche previously obscure or unknown, either by looking for data that might be expected to exist or by finding data that do not fit. So long as the source of abstract ideas is known and they are used and tested, a danger that applies to all psychological theorising can be avoided: the abstract concept will not be used as a defence against the more primitive, archaic or infantile states which it contains and represents. Because my own theory was first presented without adequate indication of the grounds on which it was based, it has so far seemed to lack adequate support. The second edition of my book went somewhere towards filling in an omission which was only too apparent to me. Since then further support has come from infant–mother observations and interesting studies have been made by combining observation with experimental work: the evidence from psychoanalysis, especially by Daniel Stern, who has organised them in terms of self theory (Stern 1985).

The difficulty of adequately conveying the kind of data that underlie abstract statements is very considerable, indeed a scheme for recording clinical data in sufficient detail has yet to be constructed. It should lie half way between the model and the longhand account which can now only be presented in part, through short extracts of incidents that crystallise the often long and painstaking work of analytic investigation. However, an account of the methods by which data are collected and assessed can help to give an impression of the range of investigation. Therefore it is my intention to summarise the methods by which data have been obtained.

The main one used here has been analytic. The reader will need to refer to other volumes if he has not already sufficient knowledge of analytic procedures as a whole; their application to childhood is allocated to a later chapter. Here only the method of reconstructing the early years will be given special consideration, since it has been the most important amongst analytic manoeuvres in child study. To analytic method direct observations of infants and children have been added.

Reconstruction

Much analytic work consists in working out in detail the infantile roots of symptoms, dreams, fantasies and behaviour; indeed ideally the analyst would like to construct a complete picture of a patient's development. This cannot, however, be done, because therapeutic considerations intervene: the patient's libidinal investment of infantile situations will begin to recede as he gets well or, if it does not, the analyst may take steps to find out why, and so is bound in the interest of his patient to frustrate his scientific interest.

The analysis of the childhood of adults first, and of small children later, was facilitated by the use of reconstructions or postulates about the childhood and infancy of a patient based on analytic material whose source is not easily recognised. Freud first used the method and his discovery of infantile sexuality and the oedipal conflict was facilitated thereby. Since then reconstructions have been extended to the first weeks of life and intra-uterine experiences.

The technique involves making postulates which can be confirmed, denied or modified by the patient. Confirmation or otherwise is arrived at in two ways. First, the reconstruction made by an analyst may lead to the emergence of a memory confirming the inference. Second, by accumulating data that point to a situation which, however, cannot be remembered. By using reconstructions alongside memories it is possible to build up a picture of a period in infancy or childhood which fits the psychology of the patient so well that it carries conviction. Only at times can these reconstructions be confirmed from sources outside the analysis.

Accounts of reconstructions can seem thin, unconvincing or vulnerable to intellectual criticism; this is partly due to the difficulty of presenting the great amount of work which precedes arriving at a reconstruction and the subsequent testing of it against any new data that emerge. In addition the affective situation in which the work is done makes intellectual considerations secondary. They must be there as a framework, but they are not the only basis for estimating the validity of a reconstruction. Ultimately their meaningfulness to the patient is the most relevant. This does not, however, necessarily mean that his acceptance of a reconstructive interpretation is always reliable. On the contrary, because of the transference situation, all sorts of statements by an analyst may be accepted or rejected just because of distortions resulting from the transference of affects on to the analyst. Only by consistent analysis of them can the significance and reliability of the patient's responses be estimated.

Validating a reconstruction is therefore a complex and difficult exercise, and before one is given credence, several different attempts may have to be made till a good fit between present and past can be achieved. Even then it will be useful if, before reconstructions are generalised, confirmation can be achieved through direct observation of children. Much of the theory of infantile sexuality has been easily substantiated, especially those parts of it that apply to relatively mature children, i.e. of between four and six years of age. But because an infant has not the means of communication available to a five-year-old child, drawing conclusions from observing babies is far more difficult. To penetrate into their feelings and the nature of their affective processes requires inference and experiment as well as simple observation.

The correlation of reconstructive interpretations with observations during the first weeks and months of life has, however, produced increasing certainty, and arising out of this are now good working hypotheses for investigating infant behaviour.

Infant and child observation

It is no longer enough to make naive records of what children do or say. These may give a shock of surprise or pleasure, be passed around for entertainment or built into traditions as to the nature of children. Today observations have been developed and collected with the aid of rigorous methods.

Because psychoanalysts succeeded in developing a meaningful genetic theory of development, the most useful observations had been made by them. To some extent that is so today but a host of others have also contributed. The following list covers those most relevant to my thesis:

1. Observations have been made of initial feeding behaviour whilst mother and infant are in hospital soon after birth. An early, beautiful example of this is recorded by Merell Middlemore.

2. Observations have been made in paediatric clinics. Amongst these those made by D.W. Winnicott were important and pioneering.
3. There have been longitudinal studies made on infants and small children. Amongst these those made in 'well baby clinics' in the United States were pioneering. They covered the ages between three months and two or three years. Others have started in infancy and continued for five or six years to nursery school. The name of Kris and his co-workers is associated with these studies, which have been combined with analysis of particular children. More recently mention must be made of Mahler's work (Mahler et al. 1975) and, of course, the monumental researches of Piaget.
4. Observations have been made at various times and in many age groups of which Spitz (1946) on analclitic depression, and on the development of 'no' and 'yes' (1957), were pioneering.
5. There has in the last two decades been a regular outburst of studies of the mother–infant relation both in Great Britain and the United States. From amongst them I single out those initiated at the Tavistock Clinic in London. Their method has been widely adopted and accepted as part of the child analytic training by the Society of Analytical Psychology. An observer visits the home and records each observation in detail without drawing conclusions. Each observation lasts one hour and is repeated each week for the first two years of extra-uterine life. The findings are then discussed each week in a seminar. The method and its findings are well described in *Closely Observed Infants* (Miller et al. 1989).
6. There have been numerous observations made under more controlled laboratory conditions, sometimes with experimental additions, particularly at Cambridge University.
7. Finally there is the sand play method first used extensively by Margaret Lowenfeld and exploited extensively by Dora Kalff and numerous analytical psychologists as a therapeutic method.

Comparative techniques

Amplification has already been considered in Chapter 1, but comparative anthropological studies have not. Erikson and Margaret Mead have been pioneers but others have followed them; these are now too numerous to single out. They will be referred to as the occasion arises.

6 MATURATION

What does it mean to say that a baby is primarily a psychosomatic unity – a self; when does this state of affairs exist and when do deintegrative–integrative sequences start and give rise to the process of maturation? I shall endeavour to present what significant knowledge we have on these subjects.

INTRA-UTERINE LIFE

It can easily be forgotten, because of the fantasies and beliefs that surround intra-uterine life, that the fertilised ovum and the foetus are, from the start, separate from their mother's body. As growth proceeds the mother's abdominal wall and the amniotic fluid contain and protect the growing infant from the outside world. He lives in an aquatic placenta and the amniotic fluid from both of which he feeds. The mother's main function is thus to contain and protect him, while she provides the raw materials for growth. Genetic inheritance can thus act to form the shape and structure of the baby's body.

Living inside the uterus is no life of bliss; it is, for instance, a noisy place; the pulsating of the abdominal aorta is very loud and sounds like an old-fashioned steam engine snorting away whilst the borborygmi must also disturb the supposed tranquillity of the womb. Such sounds will not of course be heard at first and will not have much, if any, affect on the foetus, but they must later on, when the nervous system is formed. An additional discomfort is added as the foetus grows in size: the space to live in is reduced and becomes restricted so that some of his movements seem designed to make him more comfortable. Finally it is now thought increasingly likely that his mother's emotional states affect him for good or ill, though we can only speculate on how that happens.

By five months the structuring within the brain is complete and so sense perception and motor activity will be possible, indeed arm and leg movements are easily perceptible by the mother. In addition, thumb sucking, swallowing amniotic fluid, restricted breathing 'exercises' and rather beautiful spiral body movements can all be observed. An infant can also hear sounds from outside the body wall, thus confirming the otherwise astonishing reports from mothers that their baby responds to music; Mozart being calming whilst Beethoven increases their baby's body movements. Hearing is therefore well developed before birth. It is less easy to understand how sight is so well developed after birth for there is only very diminished light in the uterus and it is usually understood that stimuli are required for the development of perception.

These examples are enough to indicate that the intra-uterine life of a baby is both rich and varied. It is a period of growth during which he prepares for birth by developing the organs (especially mouth and muscles) which he will need to use for his survival after birth. There is some evidence to believe that he initiates the birth by sending chemical messages to his mother. If that is so, it would increase the value of looking at birth as an instance of deintegration in which the violent potential of the self is expressed. This information suggests a possible answer to one question: when do deintegrative–reintegrative sequences begin? They probably do so during intra-uterine life: activity indicating deintegration, the quiescent periods suggesting reintegration.

Birth violently interrupts the infant's protected aquatic life. It is widely held that the event gives rise to prototypic anxiety, reflected in the birth and rebirth themes of archetypal fantasy. It is also regarded as a traumatic experience. I cannot agree with that except in the case of births that are excessively protracted or otherwise pathological. After birth, it is true the baby gives out a cry which probably facilitates his first breath and he exhibits a varying amount of distress, but if put in his mother's arms immediately after birth and allowed to nestle beside her there is often no further crying. Furthermore if the baby is left there for three quarters of an hour, subsequent attachment is greatly facilitated and a good relation to the mother is more easily formed.

If the idea of birth trauma can be rejected, how best to understand the amount of anxiety that the infant shows? I speculate as follows: is the anxiety due to the pain of passing down the birth canal, with massive skin stimulation and pressure moulding the head whilst there is little means of making a physical protest against all of this, combined with the shock of finding himself in a completely new environment? Alternatively, is there an internal contribution from the infant? I suggest that there may be such a contribution in that the self, to meet these external changes, deintegrates producing massive, non-specific forms of anxiety, which attack the environment. The attack contributes to the formation of such experiences as nameless dread, catastrophic chaos or terror of a black hole, especially when not reintegrated. But the infant appears to integrate his birth experience quite quickly, which birth trauma theory does not account for. To facilitate reintegration, it is important that something tangible and reliable is found by the baby after birth, especially through skin contact with his mother.

THE NURSING COUPLE

The momentous event of birth is followed by other changes which derive from the infant's need to be fed, nursed and held, all necessary for his survival in his new environment and a requirement for deintegrative–integrative sequences to take place. His mother's responsiveness to these needs leads to the establishment of a relationship between the two which is referred to as 'the nursing couple', to which both members contribute their share.

Much study has been directed to the impulses, reflexes and chemical systems which operate in the infant during the first few weeks and months of extra-uterine life, but though a healthy mother may know something about these, she does not relate to her offspring as if he were such a bundle of physiological systems but rather as a personal and individual being. In my view she thus grasps and respects her baby's real nature and his wholeness, which he and she will progressively get to know as growth proceeds. At the same time the mother recognises her baby's independence from her, which his birth has underlined. This has been a loss to her, which is made up for by fulfilling her part as one of the nursing couple. The loss often leads to a transitory depression, which probably helps to fill up the gap left by the absence of the baby inside her.

Superficially it appears as if the mother alone initiates the first feed, though it is clear that her baby soon takes a part in bringing it about. This is reported in the pioneering observations made by Call (1964) who showed that after a few feeds, if a mother holds a baby upright he goes through a behavioural sequence – approach behaviour – which, with the mother's co-operation, brings the baby to the breast. We may thus regard the mother's behaviour as facilitating a deintegration that will lead the baby to initiate actions culminating in his taking the nipple into his mouth and starting to suck. Further evidence from academic research and infant observation has accumulated showing the extent of the infant's contribution to forming the nursing couple. Many years ago it was shown by Dr Middlemore that the baby would not suck from a nipple which was deformed, and there are other examples where the initiation of breast feeding can be difficult or even impossible for some infants and their mothers.

In establishing the feeding situation the unity of the baby is disturbed by deintegrative acts, early actions of the self. The theory of deintegrates, however, presupposes a directed pattern emerging from the whole self and carrying with it features of the psychic potential in that whole self. It follows that each response (deintegrative act), would be an experience for the infant of its whole world. This state of affairs develops after some time into infantile omnipotence, a well-established feature of infantile behaviour. In this state of mind there can be no breast 'out there' (the breast has become a self-object) and the baby can only experience the breast through this self representation. This can, however, be only partly true as Call's experiment indicates. Infant–mother observation also confirms that the omnipotence is not sustained all the time. Furthermore it has long been known that the shape of the nipple can facilitate or discourage an infant in his attachment to the breast, so he has a capacity for discrimination.

Once breast feeding is established by deintegrative acts, and facilitated by the mother, part of the milk previously ingested may be regurgitated, but eventually it is followed by sleep (reintegration). It is these deintegrative acts that bring the sensory-motor systems (looking, smiling, touching) into operation and so material for ego growth is provided in the first feed and all subsequent ones as well.

It is not my intention to consider in detail what sort of consciousness an infant has at any particular stage in his development. Nevertheless I referred in a previous edition of this book to the earlier work of Spitz on this subject. He claimed (Spitz 1965) that at first perceptions were vague and global, and only at about three months could the infant recognise 'pre-objects'. He claimed that the smile of the baby depended upon the baby being presented with a schema composed of forehead, eyes and nose. It was not until seven months, he claimed, that personal recognition took place, only then had libidinal object relations been established. His studies, important as they were at the time, now seem very dated. Further, they depended upon studying what kind of consciousness a baby could have at any particular stage in his development. This is interesting but the distinction between a conscious system and an unconscious mind, in the sense that we know it in children and adults, can stand in the way of studying the baby as a whole in relation to his mother.

Massive research has been undertaken since Spitz's pioneering work and a different attitude towards infancy has emerged which places the self in the centre of the studies. Stern (1985) has assembled the work that has been done round the development of the infant's 'sense of self and others'. He does not postulate a primal self in my sense though he comes near to doing so: he studies self representation developing out of the primal self, in my sense, finding that first of all a sense of emergent self can be distinguished followed by the formation in sequence of a 'Core Self', a 'Subjective Self' and a 'Verbal Self'. There are also other findings which are relevant to my propositions. He tells us that learning about what is variant and what invariant in the environment is not just an abstract process but is essentially bound up with affective experience. Furthermore sense experience is organised in a particular way: the perceptual systems are not separated out as in adult life, so that visual and auditory messages can operate as though they are the same. This he terms a 'cross-modal transfer of information' (Stern, p.48f.). This may be considered in the light of my postulate of the primal self: it would mean that sense perceptions result from a deintegrate of the whole self in which all sense modalities were only partly distinguished.

Whatever the objects, as perceived by the infant, are like, there can be no doubt that he is object-seeking from the start of extra-uterine life. For that reason it cannot be that he exists only in a narcissistic state, nor that he is fused with, nor in a state of identity with, nor only a part of his mother's unconscious, nor that he is primarily unintegrated (c.f. Winnicott). These views I consider over-generalised perceptions of what an infant may sometimes be like or states which he may be in from time to time. When I say that a baby is object-related I mean that he can distinguish the parts of his mother he comes across from himself though I do not mean that he is conscious of so doing – that comes later. Theory of the self would suggest that he is mostly in a state which is neither conscious nor unconscious for much of the time. This structured dichotomy, so useful both descriptively and dynamically in later life, is not useful in describing the early behaviour of infants.

The kind of object the infant encounters is further suggested by my theory. Observation indicates that an infant has some clear perception of reality but that he also forms objects out of the self in relation to his environment. These objects are considered to be archetypal, in a form analagous to the schema and models of other researchers, but they represent themselves very differently from the ethnological material through which archetypes are usually identified. They can be observed in breast feeding where one breast is treated differently from the other, and in periodic attacks on the mother, or in efforts to enter into her: these all have patterned features. I find Bion's notation useful with reference to early object formation (Bion 1970): he considers that the first objects are beta elements; these are transformed into alpha elements by alpha function. Beta elements have the emotional quality of things in themselves concretely experienced, i.e. as 'accretions of stimuli'. When transformed by alpha function they can then be dreamed and thought about. These elements seem too abstract but they indicate that early objects have two forms which precede the formation of fantasies, dreams and myths, and that stimulates further observation.

One of the great changes that has come over our perception of infancy is acknowledging the way in which the infant actively attaches his mother to him. There is his inherent beauty but there are other ways he signals to her and endears himself to her, all examples of deintegrative activity, for instance smiling, cooing and looking. On the other hand he may cry, scream and protest in many ways if he is displeased. Our present understanding of infancy shows that the nursing couple is essentially interactional. In the first weeks and months the self deintegrates further. Simple discharges divide up into opposites and this enables the baby to organise his accumulating experience into 'good' and 'bad' objects. The objects producing satisfaction, such as the breast during and after a good feed, are good objects. They lead, perhaps after a period of play with his mother, to sleep and so to re-establishment of the unity of the infant. Those that do not satisfy, because they do not meet the infant's needs, felt as hunger or other bodily discomforts, are bad objects. I should add here that the infant's objects are not linked to the breast alone but soon come to be associated to a cluster of other experiences derived from his being held, cuddled, bathed, nappy-changed and looked at. He gains much experience also when he gazes about him, evacuating, ruminating or having thoughts.

Good or bad objects can be blissful or catastrophic, both of which are overwhelming. Apart from these intense experiences, the baby starts to develop ways of managing his objects, the quality of which do not necessarily depend upon their real behaviour. A short period in which the breast is absent, for instance, can lead to its becoming a bad thing and hunger can then absorb the baby completely. As the absent breast is experienced concretely, it is treated as the origin of his pain, apparently inside him. It can be got rid of by evacuating it (by, for instance, defecating or screaming). If the evacuation is not successful the breast remains completely bad and the good breast cannot be found anywhere. Consequently the infant will relate his hunger to a nourishing breast when it is presented to him and it may take considerable care on the mother's part to start a feed. I do not want to give the impression that if the mother fails the position is hopeless; for the baby has means of coping by evacuating the bad internal object through continued screaming, defecating, urinating and, surprisingly, forming a thought.

The idea of good and bad objects is linked with that of part objects (see Klein, *The Psycho-Analysis of Children*, 1932). The latter concept seems at first sight quite obvious in that an infant relates to the breast, which is only part of the mother. Later he comes to know her more and more completely or as a whole. It is, however, questionable whether an infant experiences his mother as a part object in the first place. His field of experience is after all restricted and it is only as he extends his experience and so his knowledge of her body that he recognises the breast as part of his mother. The perceptual capacity is, however, urged on by his emotional experience of the breast as sometimes satisfying and sometimes not; for if there are two breasts one can be good and the other bad. I therefore postulate that there is a period in which the infant's experience of the breast is of a whole object before it is experienced as a part object.

In paying so much attention to the relation of a baby to the breast it is important to recognise the extended sense in which the term is meant. A breast feed is not just a matter of transferring milk, it is also an experience in which a baby's relation to his mother begins to be worked out. Looking, caressing, loving, attacking and smelling are important too (whilst periods of play, perhaps with the nipple, can also be observed), but comparable intimacies and conflicts also occur in bathing and nappy changes. In this brief description of an infant's life there are long periods when he is not actively engaged with his mother. This is so in sleep and when he is in a more reflective, even contemplative, condition as if having thoughts about his experiences and making it probable that very early on it is possible to envisage elemental mental processes at work. He also soon begins to make a relation with impersonal things such as toys and other objects which he can handle or put in his mouth, such as his thumb or fist. In these ways he expands his experience progressively and so prepares the way for a life separate from his mother.

In this early period the mother's sensitive provision and care for her baby is particularly important. Although she will attend to physiological needs she treats her baby as a person – so she relates to the infant self whom she can know empathically through projective identification. Apart from conscious knowledge, unconscious memories of her own infancy can be important; inasmuch as they are good enough she can not only look after the infant as a separate person but can also put a part of herself into her baby's situation to his benefit. Thus by anticipating and meeting her infant's needs, from what were once her own needs she creates a situation by projective identification in which disturbances in her baby are made tolerable for him. This facilitates deintegrative–reintegrative sequences, and is similar to Bion's descriptions of maternal reverie whereby the mother receives the infants beta elements and drawing on her own resources makes sense of them for her infant. Moreover if her projection matches the state of her infant in detail, the infant self is thereby affirmed so that its unity is replaced by the mother–infant unit. Only a certain amount of this state seems desirable as it can make separation of the infant from the mother very difficult.

It is, however, inevitable that she frustrates her infant: some frustrations are tolerable whilst others are not so; the value of tolerable frustrations is that they compel the infant to manage his bad and good objects, especially by projection and introjection, which operate to produce a preponderance of good nourishing reserves within the self. In this way the infant's struggle leads to his gaining increasing control over his objects. His mother will help him develop his ego, and in this way his capacity for distinguishing himself from herself, and fantasies from reality. By providing reliable and empathic care, a mother thus creates the basis for feelings of trust from which an infant's sense of individual identity grows. This care is quite within the capacity of an ordinary good mother so long as she has good environmental provision and support and is not interfered with.

The picture of a 'good enough mother' can, however, easily be idealised and I will therefore end with a mother's comment on a lecture she heard which did give such a picture. She said something like this: 'It is all very well but suppose I have my husband's dinner to cook, my baby to breast feed [she will scream if not fed], my son [aged about two] crying and clinging to my skirt so as to drive me "mad" and I want to be rid of the lot!' The rough and tumble of family relationships is inevitable and desirable; indeed a mother–infant relation without some of it makes separation difficult and sometimes detrimental. In *The Psychological Birth of the Human Infant* Mahler gives an example of a mother–infant relationship which was almost ideal: this made separation very difficult and by three years the toddler's development was retarded. It is thus important to recognise not only an infant's love and hate of his mother but also the love and hate that he can evoke in her.

DEVELOPMENT AND MANAGEMENT OF PART OBJECTS

I have postulated that at first the infant experiences only whole objects, partly because of his restricted view of his mother and partly because of the nature of his emotional life. As he comes to know more of her he recognises that her breasts are only a part of her and that there are two of them. His emotional experience concomitantly distinguishes, by deintegration, that he has good and bad experiences in relation to the breast and that consequently there is a good and a bad breast separate from each other. The existence of good and bad part objects creates a situation in which a number of ways of dealing with them gradually emerge. A bad object can be projected into the breast, and then it seems that the breast is attacking the baby by biting him, though the baby has in reality bitten the breast himself. On the other hand, as the example given above of the bad breast implied, the objects can be introjected. The same processes take place with good objects: they can be projected into the breast which becomes idealised and can produce not only satisfaction but concurrently a feeling of bliss. The good breast can also be taken in, introjected, and this gives the infant more good objects inside and increases the experience of himself as good through identification of himself with the good object.

All this implies that good and bad part object experiences have become representations, and when this happens a field of consciousness has developed. At first the two kinds of object are not connected because the infant has no means of relating them to each other, but soon the ego starts to struggle with them so as to keep the good and bad objects separate. The intensity of anxiety can be very great, and has the 'all or none' quality of an omnipotent and ruthless object.

The development of the processes referred to as projection, introjection and idealisation, in later life so easily recognised as essentially psychical processes, is much more primitive and 'physical' to an infant. Thus projection can only be perceived when affective experience can be compared with reality and seen to be different from it. What this step means can be seen by reflecting that in the first place the equation of mother and self leads to states that in the adult would be called delusions. These are often called projections though, at this stage, projection is implied rather than existing, for it is only when ego growth has proceeded far enough for there to be boundaries between the infant and mother that we can speak of the ego projecting, introjecting and identifying with objects; each of these mechanisms implies the existence of two frames of reference, i.e. subject and object.

But inasmuch as all these processes seem to take place apart from ego activity and are therefore unconscious, they must first be based on archetypal structures that have deintegrated out of the self in the early stages of maturation. Each of these structures has boundaries and so can project or introject parts of themselves into others.

It is tempting to try and anatomise these early stages of maturation in a detail which can easily become misleading, because they presuppose ego structures that are improbable. The introduction of combined terms for intermediate stages has, however, proved useful: for instance projective and introjective identification have achieved increasing recognition.

Before leaving this attempt to conceptualise a primitive, pre-personal and ruthless period, it is worth trying to formulate in living bodily form the nature of two of the three dynamic processes as they are experienced by babies: introjection is eating, hearing, seeing, breathing in; projection is excreting, spitting, regurgitating, vomiting and breathing out. Identification by contrast has no physical correlate, being a development of the first vestigial experiences of reality.

Further attempts have been made to understand the nature of early objects. They must stem from the red or infra-red end of the archetypal spectrum (Fordham 1985a) but Bion has further differentiated beta elements, giving rise through the action of alpha function to alpha elements. It is a very abstract formula which is designed to avoid speculation. I find it useful in differentiating data which are presented in case material and infant observation. Both beta elements refer to states before fantasy, dream, myth and speech.

The transitional object

The first months have so far been directed to the deintegrative archetypal aspects of the mother–infant unit and the rudimentary efforts of the ego to control good and bad part objects on the basis of patterns derived from the dynamics inherent in the nature of the self. The description has lately been extended by Winnicott in a way that is significant for analytical psychologists.

It has long been known that small children sometimes become attached to objects which seem to be essential to their well-being. These may be anything from a bit of rag or stuff to a doll, particularly a soft one. They are treated as possessions and attempts to remove them are vigorously, even violently, resisted, as if children's existence in some sense depended upon them. That the object itself is needed shows that it is not part of the child's inner world nor does it represent a part of the mother or other libidinal object in the external world, for it is, in reality, controllable, and has multiple significance.

The transitional object, as Winnicott calls it, is conceived to originate during periods in which the mother is around and the baby is secure and comfortable. Then the baby may use the breast, or a bit of cloth that gets into his mouth, to play with and to create illusions (or delusions) which become meaningful. Thus the transitional object links with part objects, the nipple, skin, etc., which can be used to produce satisfaction in terms of libidinal need, but which are not doing so. The transitional object is not a substitute for libidinal and aggressive objects but is rather an early attempt at self representation and so may be the first symbolisation of all. In its development the transitional object acquires archaic characteristics, and in it are found all kinds of part object (i.e. oral, anal and phallic) representations. These are, however, drawn into the object in an attempt to extend the self representation by the ego and the integrative action of the self during quiet and secure periods between deintegrative activity. Here it is apparent that the early stages of psychic objectification are to be found and the 'spiritual' pole of the archetype is being used and developed; indeed Winnicott locates the source of cultural processes here (for further on this topic c.f. p.119f.).

WHOLE OBJECTS

Round about seven months, simple observation and experiment combine to show that a radical change takes place: the infant recognises his mother as a libidinal object (Spitz 1965) and he shows more explicit evidence that separation from her is distressful. Before this time it seems easier to substitute another woman for her, but now the baby can show signs of anaclitic depression (Spitz 1946) if his mother is absent for too long, and especially in crisis periods. Independently psychoanalysts have also dated changes at about this time: Klein formulated a theory of the depressive position; she held that it began at about four months and culminated at six months. Winnicott called it the stage of concern but cautiously refused to date it.

The change is like one from 'madness' and unintegration to sanity and integration; it is a step from part object life to living with whole objects, i.e. persons. During it the sense of reality increases to make recognition of the infant's dependent situation clearer. Concurrently the inner world – already made possible partly by perceptual developments, but also by earlier introjection of sufficient good omnipotent objects which have ensured that they will not be overcome by the bad ones – is given increasing definition.

The change from part to whole object relations is especially significant because it means that objects previously felt to be either good or bad, blissfully satisfying or catastrophically frustrating and persecuting, can now be recognised as the same object. Consequently the baby becomes concerned lest, in his angry or greedy attacks, he damages or destroys his mother's good breast when he feels it is also bad. And he can now feel that this has happened and recognise his need for his mother's continued existence.

At this point he may mobilise some of the old feelings and, by denying that the breast is good and bad, make an illusion that it is only bad, and so apparently make it safe to triumph over. But this illusion does not really work, and so his triumph does not bring comfort but restless and excited exaltation.

The defence in his triumph (manic defence) is made against another sequence which derives from the infant pining, feeling concern, a prototype of guilt, which leads to his being overwhelmed by a kind of depression not, however, to be confused with its adult equivalent. If he does feel this, he has yet to make the next step in discovery: he can repair the damage. He can feel that there is a cavity or hole that he has made in his mother during his greedy attack on her and that this can be filled up, and his mother restored. When he does so, he begins all those feelings that become 'being sorry about' and 'wanting to make better' the harm that has occurred as the result of some accidental or deliberate damage of which he has been the cause. Feelings of guilt, sadness and the capacity to make reparation all originate in this period.

I have given this outline of developments in infancy relying mostly on Melanie Klein's work. Over the years, as the result of more clinical work and the findings of infant observation, I have come to realise that neither the period in which part objects predominate (in the paranoid–schizoid position, according to Klein) nor the depressive position are to be found in pure culture. Much less organised patterns usually predominate.

Sometimes there is an idea that the paranoid-schizoid position is followed by the depressive position, as though they were two stages. In my experience they are not stages in the sense of being superseded, they are rather achievements which persist throughout life and have a large archetypal content. I consider Bion has done us a service by defining the formula Ps<–>Dp to indicate that either position can be found in pure culture but that there are many examples, indeed probably most, which show a mixture of persecution and depression. Nonetheless, the model here presented has a useful orienting function and I have consequently preserved the account almost intact from the previous edition.

Symbol formation

Usually symbolic images increasingly replace concrete object representation. The increase in the baby's sense of reality runs concurrently with the formation of his self image and so his capacity to build up his inner world. His objects are no longer mother–self objects but his own, and his self images are distinguished from external object representations. This important step is an essential part of the formation of whole objects. Concurrently the baby's feelings about his mother and himself become distinguished in the formation of external objects and the symbolic images of his inner world.

The progression to symbolic representation has, however, a different aspect brought about by the formation of transitional objects. They do not belong to the inner world nor to the outer, but refer to or combine both. They are therefore between the two and make room for symbolism of a different kind, which bridges reality and the inner world. In the first place they participate in the concreteness of the part objects but it is known that they are important in learning processes, play and fantasy. Therefore in the symbolising processes they become less attached to objects and more to plastic forms of expression and hence later are culturally significant.

Conclusion

Enough has now been said to draw a conclusion relevant to the general theory of analytical psychology. The self in which interrelated omnipotent objects have developed has become represented in an organised central personal ego which reflects its wholeness and contains good and bad objects. Though there is an essential imbalance, in that the good objects are sufficient to predominate over the bad ones, the structures have been developed which can render future steps in separation sad but rewarding.

IDENTITY

Maturation has so far been thought of as taking place during the oral (nutritional) phase, when the baby is primarily concerned with his mouth as a source of excitement, satisfaction, frustration, anxiety, and the focus of his growing perceptual world. His deintegrative drives, reflected in hunger and greed, were focused on feeding and his ego was occupied in gaining progressive mastery over them. But much more has gone on than feeding; greater control has been progressively achieved over skeletal musculature mainly employed in the service of exploration, yet whose activity, often violent biting and scratching, is a major source of destructive fantasies. Further, anal and urethral activities have played a part which has been touched on but not developed. As in feeding, the interplay of libidinal and aggressive energies has given rise to anxieties about the effect of excreta on the infant's mother and on himself. On the one hand there has been pleasure and satisfaction in the release of internal tensions: faeces and urine were felt as parts of the self which can be good objects, gifts given in gratitude for the love and care resulting in comfort when distress and pain threatened to become intolerable. On the other hand there have been fears of drowning, poisoning and destroying his mother and himself with their imagined violence, which at first plays ruthlessly on her and his own body and then, as the objects become recognised as both good and bad, feelings of concern, sadness, guilt, and wishes to make reparation develop and symbolisation begins to take place.

The importance of control over excreta takes its place in relation to control over feeding and the expansion of the infant's perceptual field, his reality sense and especially his inner world located inside his body. His excreta take a special place in expressing his being a person with a skin surface that defines what is inside and what is outside. Though he can exert little control over his internal bodily functions he can increasingly decide what he takes in and what he extrudes. His sense of self is increased as his body image becomes established and it may be abstracted, imagined, symbolised or broken up and apparently dissolved. But in health it persists once control over excreta, feeding and musculature has been mastered.

The essentials of a self representation in the ego are well given in this simple paradigm of the body image. To complete the significant dynamism of its life other activities need adding: crying, screaming, spitting, at first release activities, become communicative; incorporative activities, like holding and clinging, are now increasingly recognised as essential to infant well-being and so as self feelings.

Vision occupies a special place in perception, and in establishing object constancy there arises the feeling of being one and the same person in space and time. As the distance percept starts to function at the first feed, so this leads to exploring the external world and forming the basis for recognising that objects continue to exist in their physical absence. But object constancy is not only visual, it applies both to objects outside the skin surface and to the person of the infant himself, who in the setting of his mother's care and empathy discovers his own continuity of being; it was there in the first place as the self in its transcendent sense, but was unrepresented and has to be discovered by the ego gradually, piece by piece.

The next steps in self mastery are arrived at by exploring the external world. An infant has up to now been dependent upon parts of it being presented to him directly or indirectly by his mother, except in respect of seeing and hearing. To be sure, he can start putting food into his mouth when it is put near enough to him, and he has learnt that expressions of rage and pining will result in objects being provided for him, and he can fantasy magical omnipotent control over them, but it is only when he can first crawl that he can in reality increase the accuracy and range of his discovery in which up to now only his eyes and ears were of much use.

One other motor activity has still to be mastered: it is speech. Once achieved, the infant becomes in all essentials viable – a fully communicating and basically independent person.

THE 'SEPARATION–INDIVIDUATION PHASE'

When a child has become mobile, first by crawling and then walking, he has reached the toddler stage. From now on he becomes physically far more independent of his mother: he can play with toys of his own choosing, he can get those that he wants without having them brought to him, and he can manipulate a wide variety of objects with a skill that rapidly increases.

Normally a toddler plays on his own for a restricted period and cannot tolerate his mother's absence for long without signs of distress. If he plays on his own he will tend to return to her from time to time, clamber on to her lap and then climb down to continue his play. Soon mother's absence can be tolerated and the presence of a substitute will do and so on till at nursery school age he can happily join a group.

These manifestations of progressive independence are also due to the child's use of toys as symbolic representations of ideas and fantasies which facilitate independence and develop social relations by providing an objective medium of communication. These developments at the toddler stage have been referred to as the separation–individuation phase by Mahler et al. (1975) and are so called because they end the 'symbiotic phase' of identity between mother and infant. Her formulation draws attention to the increased capacity for mobility, as cogently expressing individuation in action. There is also clear evidence that the infant is developing his ego functions in his independent activities, which in themselves will soon no longer need his mother's presence. Certainly there are many signs of identification besides individuating processes. The need of the infant to reunite with his mother is still evident between his exploratory activities, but in this period there can be no doubt that primary identity, or, as Jung called it alternatively, *participation mystique*, is progressively dissolving. The infant's symbolic life is also becoming better established along with his greater mastery of reality. It is a period of increasingly stable integration. Early on deintegrative processes predominated in growth; gradually they did so less, and then with the development of an inner world true symbolisation began and the reality sense became greater; separation–individuation processes were well under way. By two years it may be said that ego growth has gone far enough for integrative processes to be stabilised over against primitive integrative-deintegrative sequences. The individuating processes that first began when whole object relations developed are now clear for all to see. Jung's definition that individuation is 'the process of forming and specialising the individual nature . . .' and 'the development of consciousness [the ego] out of the original state of identity' clearly applies.

The use of the term individuation in relation to infancy has led to protests that this is not the same as Jung's usage, and so as not to cause confusion Henderson (1967) proposed that it would be better to refer to 'the individuating processes', reserving the single word to indicate the processes that Jung worked on so much in the later part of life. The only objection I have to Henderson's proposal is that it makes for cumbersome nomenclature and makes it seem as if the dynamic processes in each case are essentially different – this is not my position.

THE OEDIPAL CONFLICT

The next critical phase in maturation is the oedipal conflict. It is the period during which the basis for subsequent heterosexual life is laid down and in which genital feelings, impulses and fantasies mature and make themselves conscious.

The aspect of this period to which I want to draw attention is its importance in the child's growing sense of his identity. The earliest identity conflicts begin in the pre-oedipal period; they become increasingly evident during the toddler stage and they culminate in the oedipal phase because the child's feelings about himself as male or female are thrown into relief.

A boy or a girl, given tolerant and trustworthy parents, will have realised the existence of sexual differences before this time; penis envy in the little girl and penis pride in the boy, allied to castration anxieties in both, will have become conscious so long as the parents' attitude is perceptive and tolerant. If it is inadequate the discoveries may be withheld or made secretively and indirectly. In the oedipal period the establishment of genital primacy and the rivalries with and jealousies of the parent of the same sex become central. Increasing weight and poignancy is given to fantasies, feelings and impulses related to the physical relationship between the parents. The primal scene, first believed to record the child witnessing his parents during sexual intercourse, was later recognised as representing not only the real event but also the child's fantasies about sexual union. This discovery means that the situation is an archetypal one. It corresponds to the conjunction that has been studied intensively by Jung (C.W.14) as a central feature of individuation. The union of opposites to which it leads has, according to him, almost endless representations, abstract, archaic and sexual. To a child the primal scene comprises almost any situation in which his parents are in reality or fantasy exclusively occupied with each other to the exclusion of himself. He adapts himself to this situation either by attacking them and trying to separate them or by putting himself, either in play or in fantasy, in the position of one or other or both of them.

If maturation proceeds normally the situation leads to conflicts centring round a genital position. Alongside progression there are periodic regressions in which earlier experiences revive and lead to fantasies and speculations based on them: parents may be conceived as feeding each other or enjoying sensory pleasure in excretory activities, and frequently bizarre combinations are imagined. As with earlier sexual 'discoveries' the child's conflicts may be largely unconscious; indeed whether they become conscious or no depends to a large extent on whether his parents are aware of what is going on and understand it too.

The satisfactory outcome of this frequently complex situation is brought about by a realignment of identifications. If earlier maturation processes have gone forward smoothly enough, identification with the parent of the same sex becomes firmly established. Masturbation anxieties and guilt are increased and this leads on to the repressive mastery of the libidinal drives.

The importance of this period for identity formation is crucial. By identification the child's sexual affects are organised into patterns of behaviour and accompanying fantasies, which accord with his body image and his physical inheritance. Furthermore these patterns are allied through his parents with the collective matrix, conscious and unconscious, in which the family lives. In this process earlier identifications with the opposite sex remain but they are built in to the child's inner world. The oedipal conflict strongly reinforces the establishment of anima and animus figures which lie ready, as it were, to be projected in the love relationships of adolescence. It is here that the main trends henceforward are directed towards social adaptation on which Jung laid so much stress when he emphasised the sexual and adaptive aims of young people. He was justified in doing so because of the intensity of his study of the introverting processes of later life. But there are really no grounds for believing that the social implications in the identifications that resolve oedipal conflicts are the whole picture. The increase in the child's sense of his own identity is indeed witness to the activity of individuating processes at work, or, to put it in another way, the alignment of his sexual behaviour and fantasies with his impulses and his body image increase his capacity for true self-expression. If the ego is strengthened the underlying wholeness of the self is not necessarily made inaccessible.

In support of the idea that one-sided development is necessary and inevitable, the theory of repression can be invoked. This defence, however, belongs to the oedipal conflict and leads to sexual latency which only continues till adolescence. So long as this is brought about internally and its internal function is not masked by personal and social pressures it becomes part of the individual's means of development during latency. Defences originate when deintegration of the self brings opposites into being and when the infant ego's struggle to establish his good objects against the bad ones starts. The conflict develops into castration anxiety when the oedipal phase is reached. Repression is therefore one way of managing internal conflict. It does not apply when sexual maturity is reached anyway. However, if one defence is going to be invoked to support a questionable theory, what about all the other ones? If they are all included then individuation would mean doing away with essential ego functions, which is not how it is conceived.

LATENCY AND ADOLESCENCE

With the passing of the oedipal conflict all the essential structures of later development have been laid down; each develops further in extensity, richness and complexity: each enters into new combinations and is applied in different fields.

From now on the extent of consciousness grows and is

consolidated in the development of activities outside the family, most of all in school. During this period the persona differentiates and the child discovers how to take more part in society and find his level in it.

At adolescence this relative stability is disrupted by the maturation of the child's sexuality. Its effects will be taken up later in Chapter 8, for a significant impact of adolescent turbulence, which properly speaking does not belong to childhood, is on the social aspects of family life and on society itself.

7 The Family

Maturation can only proceed fully in a good enough environment, and that means a family life based on a good enough marriage. There is no room for perfectionism here and the inevitability of conflict in marriage is well expressed in the symbolic formula that male and female are opposites. Where there are opposites there is conflict; a marriage without it is suspect. Everybody understands that conflict between parents and children is inevitable, but conflicts between parents, if worked out, are equally an expression of vitality in the marriage relation.

It would be mistaken to claim that *any* conflict is desirable; it is rather its nature that is important both quantitatively and qualitatively. Open destructive conflict between parents is bad for children, but absence of conflict in so-called 'happy' marriages can be damaging as well, especially if the happiness is unreal, idealised and kept up at the expense of instinctual life.

An example of how such a 'happy' marriage damaged a child can be seen in its long-term result. A young woman was one of four sisters none of whom married and all of whom fell in love with men who either did not return their love or who were already married. At first it seemed that the married life of her parents had been good; there were no open conflicts, there was harmony, and the daughter was fond of her father who returned her affection, so that she believed herself to be the favourite child, as each of her sisters believed also. It turned out, however, that the father had maintained his stability at great cost to himself and his instinctual life, as he told her shortly before his death. His wife had colluded with him in this and as a result the stage at which a daughter idealises her father could not develop or change on to a more realistic basis, and so her sexuality remained infantile. As a result all adult erotic experience was frustrated by the image of her father interposing itself in her relationships with men.

This example illustrates Jung's thesis that the unlived life of parents becomes the burden of their children, or, in more technical terms, the psychopathology of parents becomes introjected by their children. The formula has many facets, for it makes a great difference at what stage in development the destructive influence of parents is most felt. The examples in the literature of analytical psychology mainly stem from post-oedipal identifications, when the solution of the parents' conflict situation brings relief to the child whose ego has developed sufficiently to resolve the trauma once its cause is removed. But the damage begins earlier in infancy; if an infant is inadequately held, fed, cared for, the result is far more serious and even catastrophic.

The negative formula about parents and children can be related profitably to another proposition, that in nursing an infant and bringing up a child the parents recapitulate their own infancy and childhood. In doing so opportunity is provided to relive and resolve, with their child, developmental failures or deviations resulting from their own past. It is only when this redevelopment fails that it brings about impingements or damage to a child because no modification is possible in the parents' affective life and a traumatic situation persists by reinforcement over and over again.

Marriage can be achieved for varying motives, but the ones of especial interest to analytical psychologists are those that stem from the identifications of the couple established in the course of their own maturation. They derive from various levels but the way in which the oedipal situation of the potential mother and father has been worked through is the most important. To put it very briefly, it is necessary for a husband and wife to reflect sufficiently the characteristics of the grandparents of the opposite sex. Too great a similarity creates infantile reactions just as too much difference makes mutual adaptation excessively difficult. The special reason for taking up this idea derives from Jung's formulations about the meaning of marriage customs in primitive tribes. He claims (c.f. Jung C.W.16, p.224f.), following Layard, that they are structured to ensure a proper compensatory interchange; they are a compromise between endogamous and exogamous tendencies. The former consolidate family ties, the latter lead to group solidarity and ongoing spiritual life. Too much of one and too much of the other lead to undesirable consequences, because either the family will become an anti-social unit (because it is satisfying in itself) or it will not receive sufficient libido to make it stable.

Jung's thesis (ibid., p.225f.) includes in it the idea that marriage depends largely upon the mutual projection of unconscious archetypal forms, the animus and the anima. Besides identifications with the personal parents of the same sex which take place during maturation, Jung held that they represent an archetypal substrate into which the identifications are built. The archetype is expressed in typical fantasies of what men, in the case of a woman, or a woman in the case of a man, ideally ought to be like and assumes that human beings are functionally bisexual. Marriage is consolidated by each partner carrying enough of these archetypal projections, which only gradually get withdrawn as each partner needs to form more and more realistic appreciation of the other. This simple statement about marriage is sufficient for present purposes. In reality it is a combination, relatively simple in biological terms, rendered extremely complex by the range of personal and social factors influencing and combining in it. For the present its effectiveness will be taken for granted and so the following discussion assumes a good enough marriage for children to be raised in. Its aim is to indicate the effects children have upon, and the benefits they receive from, their parents.

Family life begins when a wife becomes pregnant. Then she starts to withdraw some of her libido from the outside world and concentrates it on the changes in her body and the baby that is growing inside her. At first she pursues her day-to-day activities as before, but as she becomes more and more dependent and in need of so becoming, the stability of her relation to her husband is tested.

The increased demands made on him derive from her need for him to participate in the pregnancy by doing what he can to make her physical burden less. But just as she becomes physically dependent so does she also become emotionally vulnerable and in need of his care and protection. All this will be well enough understood by a couple who can trust each other because they have come from good enough families themselves and have memories of how their own parents behaved and how they themselves reacted to their mothers' pregnancy and the birth of another baby. Under these conditions their own built-in instincts will be reliable.

When labour began it was customary to exclude the father till birth had taken place. It was reinforced by medical care which aimed to make birth safe for mother and baby, and so the father, as a complicating person, was kept out of the way so that full medical care could be provided. Nowadays, however, antenatal care has made labour increasingly safe, and if parents want to be together there is no reason why they should not be and so preserve continuity of experience between them. There are techniques of 'natural childbirth' which include the father and show that in a good marriage labour can be made easier.

INFANCY

Once the baby is born the mother is instinctively prepared to meet his needs, given the support of her husband, and she relates to her infant through primary maternal preoccupation. Winnicott used this phrase to describe the capacity of a mother to become absorbed in her infant during the last weeks of pregnancy and the first weeks of extra-uterine life. In this way she becomes sensitised to the absolute needs of her baby and indeed at once starts not only satisfying but also anticipating them. It is a period during which the baby has little means of orientation and so the failure to meet a need easily becomes catastrophic. There is growing evidence that during this period the basis is being made for the infant to form the first self representation. Winnicott, from whom this formulation derives, has a different notation because he does not use the self concept in my way. He contends that if the mother does not provide a good enough environment a self does not form, and a false self replaces it. Lately Meltzer has emphasised the importance of the beautiful mother and her beautiful baby and its complex implications (Meltzer and Harris Williams 1988).

The late weeks of pregnancy, going on to the first weeks of life, are thus crucial for the baby's further development. There is a natural sequence here: the mother's increasing focus on the baby inside her, leading to birth, followed by primary maternal preoccupation. Clearly a mother who has carried the baby inside her is the best one to manage the period after birth, and so is the best person to ensure the formation of true self representations in her baby. Much can be done to make up failures by what is ordinarily called 'spoiling', but it cannot truly be remedied.

A consequence of primary preoccupation is that the father is further deprived of libido previously invested in him. It is usual not to think how he responds as particularly important, but this is not so and therefore he has been included all through my account. Of course there are primary and secondary gains for him: pride and satisfaction in his wife and the baby, and new motives for exertion in his work to keep their material existence secure. He can also draw on maternal identifications and become motherly when providing security for his wife and baby and leaving them to find out more about each other without interference. Perhaps so little attention has been paid to what he does because it seems so obvious and because his seems so much the lesser achievement, but all the same his emotional reliability and stability are tested through and through, and so the family undergoes stress when the first baby arrives which will not be repeated in the same way again.

Once the early phase has been worked through the mother can recognise that her baby is established in relation to her. From now on she can safely begin to frustrate him, for the baby will be able to grasp what this means and react with increasing reliability by crying and other expressions of rage, thus giving signs that he is hungry or suffering from other forms of discomfort. Based on her own early experience she has acquired a reliable basis for knowing what emotions her baby can begin to manage and what becomes destructive; at the same time she can get to know the length of time that her infant, when awake, can tolerate her absence.

It is the baby's self that his mother first gets to know. Rudiments of an ego, however, are soon clearly perceptible and it rapidly grows, particularly in early play between feeds and through successful management of tolerable frustration.

This attempt to describe, in outline only, how a mother establishes the nursing couple implies a degree of necessary regression. Through this she can empathise with her baby and develop herself if necessary, but it does not include the medley of affects to which her baby will subject her: she will need to participate in feelings of being sucked dry, bitten, eaten up 'cannibalistically', rejected, insulted, assaulted, as well as loved, adored and ravished. All this rich variety of experience must evoke hate as well as love in her, and so her own infantile feelings will be roused and earlier management crises in her life are liable to be evoked.

This picture of mothering is intended to introduce an aspect of a mother's nature, instinctive, non-rational, half-conscious, yet reliable. It is an aspect of what Jung called eros, whose praises he sang in such glowing terms, especially in *Memories, Dreams, Reflections* (1963, p.325f.). His praise tends, however, to obscure the realistic and non-mythological eros which a mother lives. The stresses to which she is subjected make it understandable if she needs help. Some mothers require more, others less, so if a mother cannot achieve maternal preoccupation there is no point in refraining from finding substitutes. Idealisation of motherhood cannot be justified; if breast feeding is not tolerable a bottle can be used and helpers can be introduced in such a way that mothers are not prevented from doing what they are able and fitted to do.

Just as women have varying capacities for adapting to their babies so also fathers differ in their ability for providing the support and care of their wives – for taking over the baby for a time, cooking, helping to get feeds ready when there, and so forth. If a mother's own instinctual and infantile life is tested so is the father's: for him this period can evoke envy and jealousy which he needs to know about and if necessary allow for by actively recognising his limitations and getting the support and practical help for his wife which he may not be able to provide.

OEDIPAL CONFLICTS

So far the father has been in the background – a sort of essential participating observer providing a secure home and other support for his wife. But this is not always the case and indeed, in recent times, an increasing number of fathers have come to participate in pre-labour instruction and in labour itself.

If that is done it throws into relief how intense the impact of the baby can be, leading to what Greenberg (1985) has well termed 'paternal engrossment'. That can reach almost delusional intensity: he can feel that it is he, not the mother, who has produced the baby! That was, however, only the exception but it illustrates the kind of less exaggerated feeling which birth can arouse. Optimally his experience leads to a closer relation with his wife and an increased sense of responsible caring for both mother and infant.

As development proceeds, especially during second or further pregnancies and the consequent birth of further children, the elder ones will turn to him as some of the mother's libido is partially withdrawn from them. Though right from the start the father can have an intimate relation with his child, his importance is greatly enhanced when the oedipal triangular conflicts intensify. The drives mobilised in the child with particular intensity are ambivalent, actively sexual and aggressive, and can rouse comparably intense responses in the parents. Knowledge about the jealousy and rivalry which children feel towards the parent of the same sex, and also guilt over genital excitement with concurrent castration anxieties, can go some way towards helping, but in affective crises intellectual knowledge is unfortunately a broken reed.

Jung's position on infantile sexuality has often been much criticised and with some justification, because his ideas on how to understand the facts vacillated within wide limits. Occasionally he went so far as to say that he viewed the subject from the position of the parents as if infantile sexuality was an introjective phenomenon. He never elaborated this position, so it is not known what he really meant. However, his exaggerated statement is valuable because it includes parents' affective life in the oedipal situation and probably refers to the observation that conflicts between them can lead on the one hand to compulsive sexual manifestation in their children, or on the other to virtually complete suppression in the child of direct sexual feelings, impulses or fantasies.

Anxiety on the parents' part is common because children can rouse sexual feelings in them by their behaviour. If Jung's position cannot be sustained, yet much too little attention is given to the parents' part in oedipal conflicts and surprisingly little has been recorded about it. It is not discussed openly, no doubt because of the incest taboo, which presupposes that parents act out their sexual wishes if not supported by social sanctions. But if sexual maturation means anything it could be taken as a sign of maturity if the children can succeed in exciting their parents. Far from leading to perversions it would be an indication of health so long as it be recognised as part of the oedipal conflict pattern, in which libidinal drives are inherently checked by castration anxieties and guilt. It takes a strong ego to manage the drives, and it can only be done if the sexual life between parents is healthy and they have participated in their child's libidinal life, recognising that frustration of it has an essential part in maturation. Any infantile anxieties on the parents' part can be ruthlessly sought out by their children, and from this stems often distressing infantile jealousy which can be overlooked and so leads to recrimination between the parents.

The oedipal situation is the culmination of a child's development and so cannot be thought of in isolation. The form it takes depends on earlier vicissitudes of the parent–child relation, and its successful resolution depends once again on the instinctual health of the parents. This is the important element in Jung's overstatement.

Alongside the libidinal developments at this period aggression towards the parent of the same sex, expressed in rivalry and death wishes, comes to the fore with the combination of the latter in sadism and masochism. To this also the same principle applies. Management of death wishes is perhaps more important because it is essential that the parent behaves in such a way as to support the child's concurrent admiration and trust, and so foster the identifications which will lead to repression and to the child's ongoing development.

ADOLESCENCE AND AFTER

The loosening of identifications and the growing independence of the adolescent places strains on the parents and once again tests the durability of the marriage.

Ideally a couple should be equally matched and so complement each other, but this is never the reality. At the beginning of this chapter the importance of similarities and differences in history of parents was stressed, and many changes will have taken place in the course of bringing up children, especially if it is understood that they themselves will need to change progressively as maturation proceeds.

Under favourable conditions a father's manliness will be reinforced and the wife's motherliness also. However, this can only happen if projections have taken place concurrently. In a mature personality aspects of the self are deintegrated into archetypal structures which, in the context of a family, are defined as the child archetype, the anima in the father, and the animus in the mother. Each of these archetypes is a system of relationship to the opposite sex and children, and the degree to which and the form in which they are projected depends upon the maturity of the adult. The less mature the more idealised and omnipotent will they be, so the more conflict-work will be necessary to sustain the marriage, because more infantile trends need to be worked through and resolved.

Many years ago Jung (C.W.17, p.189ff.) introduced a useful formulation. He laid emphasis on inequalities in the personalities of the married couple: one can be more complex and differentiated and gifted than the other. He noticed that the more complex of the pair was the less satisfied by the other, who was content if fascinated and contained. If this disparity is not worked on it provides a basis for disturbances in the marriage which start from the more complex person. He or she will look elsewhere for the satisfactions he/she does not get from his/her wife/husband. A particular tendency is for the anima or animus to become projected and this leads to love affairs outside marriage.

His formulation tended to leave out the degree of maturity of the individuals concerned which means, in terms of maturation as conceived in this book, the stability of the inner world and so of inner resources. Whilst complexity and richness of personality are one element, the other is the capacity for stability and the deployment of abilities in a profitable manner. In other words, the more stable and complex personality need not be a disruption to family life.

The frequency with which one partner is partially contained in the other is often emphasised by adolescence and its sequelae, which will throw differences more clearly into relief. The parents are progressively thrown back on each other, and their relation changes from a biological to an increasingly psychological and personal one. The change increases the necessity for the parents to withdraw projections that may have worked perfectly well up to now and will involve alterations in libidinal interests of quite an intense kind. Perhaps this applies more to the mother than the father, but this is not always so, and in any case leads to a renewed testing of inner resources and the development of abilities. The latter can be expressed in the mother's taking up some kind of work.

However, though adolescence marks a change in family life, it is by no means the end of it. Parents are still required from time to time, and when their children marry they will become grandparents and so instinctual satisfactions are still available.

Adolescence, however, ends intimate and continuous family

life and starts a process to which Jung paid particular attention, and during which he noted particularly strong individuating processes. He studied this period of middle and old age, to which individuation classically belongs. Certainly the second half of life had been given insufficient attention when he wrote, and to give it meaning he was fully justified in almost confining individuation to it. However, individuating processes in the sense of developing consciousness by paying attention to and activating inner resources and so making projections flexible and capable of being integrated is a continuous process.

So far the need for further individuation has been considered in terms of the need for parents to gain a more realistic understanding of each other's needs by withdrawal of aspects of the animus and the anima. Besides them, however, there is the child archetype which is a more complete self representation (c.f. C.W.9, 1, p.151ff.). As children grow up the withdrawal of the group of structures and functions expressed in this archetype will evoke further individuating processes. Functions that have become specialised will need revaluation in the light of the needs of the personality as a whole. For this reason family life can be understood as a means not only of satisfying biological (instinctual) needs, but also as a way of realising individuating processes in the personalities of the parents. The adolescence of children is a testing time for how far the parents have been able to use their combined life for maturation of their own selves, how far they have adapted parenthood to the growing needs of their children, and how far they will be able to continue to make their lives meaningful when family ties cease to be the centre of their libidinal investments.

8 THE SOCIAL SETTING

Jung's concept of the collective unconscious has so far been used to cover the sum of the archetypes. However, he also applied it to the structure of society; more specifically its unintegrated shadow aspect.

As part of group life society has developed ways of representing archetypal functioning in myths, religious observances, some art, politics and the law. In all these the archetypal patterns are relatively conscious and contribute to forming cultural patterns. But no society has represented all the needs and aspirations of its individual members and those not represented remain primitive and largely unconscious. In the aggregate it is they that form the shadow of the group and comprise the collective unconscious.

The unrepresented archetypes do not appear in ordinary social life, and so the majority are not aware of them. If, however, the prevailing culture pattern is unstable, and today this state of affairs predominates, then the unconscious archetypes become active and will become vaguely apparent in social discontent. They can lead, if their import be grasped by enough individuals, to the formation of groups advocating social reforms, religious change, new developments in art, and the like. In the course of time, and if circumstances are favourable, the groups grow and the ideas they represent, whether religious, political, intellectual or aesthetic, get assimilated into the community and some change in the culture pattern results.

Jung was particularly interested in the dreams and fantasies of individuals expressing incipient collective change (c.f. C.W.10) and, combining these with his theory and the knowledge of the history of religions he had acquired, he set the dreams of his patients in their mythological context. His very elaborate researches led him to make interpretations of major trends in civilisation and he spotlighted self symbols as indicating a sort of group individuation process going on at the present time (c.f. C.W.11, p.355ff.).

His researches have never been developed far by his followers. In the present context they provocatively demand investigation into the origin of collective representations in infancy and childhood; it is to the study of infantile origins that this chapter is devoted.

Though it is true that infants and small children can take part in and influence the formation of their environment, it is not until adolescence that children are sufficiently independent to make much impact on society; then it is their identity conflicts that become dynamically acute as they struggle to find their place in society. The increase in their often distressing rebelliousness arises in part from ongoing trends and as such is valuable. New alliances are being formed and in the process the boy or girl can come into relation with the shadow of social life and so the outrageousness of adolescent behaviour sometimes becomes a scandal. In this state of affairs regression is apparent and the relationship patterns between infant and mother are revived to become expressed in confusion and disorientation.

The regressive element is not only negative, as this account might suggest, for it establishes continuity in impersonal life and, when integrated, contributes to establishing the identity feelings of the adolescent in the expanding social context towards which he is moving away from his family. An adolescent has a long development behind him which does not disappear. He has, it is true, acquired experience in school, but this is only partly an adequate introduction to the larger world which makes many impersonal demands on him. The roots of the adolescent's uncontrollable turbulence lie, then, in infancy, when his mother and, later, other members of the family comprised his 'society'; it was in relation to them that the prototype of later patterns of behaviour were laid down.

In all the early periods, maturation processes pressed him away from pre-personal ruthless drives towards forming perceptions of himself and his mother as a person about whom he has felt concern; now at adolescence the pre-personal structures revive in response to the less personal roles he is expected to fulfil. So the infantile roots are needed if he is to find his identity in new patterns of living. Omnipotent fantasies result in attacks on parents and on society that stem from the manic defences of infancy, the source of heroes and heroines. Depressive episodes, depersonalising, hysterical and splitting processes in the ego are not at all infrequent and often constitute a kind of 'normal insanity'. The ruthlessness characteristic of these states is proverbial and when they predominate an adolescent needs support and a kind of indirect holding such as a mother provides for her infant in crises, rather than the direct control of discipline which easily provokes more rebellion.

An adolescent comes into direct contact with the culture pattern and the collective unconscious. In a very different way and right from the beginning as an infant he has been influenced indirectly by the society in which his family lives. It was expressed in collective attitudes to infants and infancy, in the methods used to care for him and the provisions made for education later on. Then he did not grapple with them directly as he does now, and will in later life, but much depends on the outcome whether early influences are related to and how he is expected to behave now.

The predominating customs surrounding birth and early infant care were not determined either by his or his parents' needs. It used to be widely held that the relationship between mother and father must be interrupted by the birth of the baby: either the mother went into hospital, from which her husband would be excluded except as a visitor after the birth, or else, if the birth took place at home, doctor and midwife took charge often to the exclusion of the father. A common regimen used to be to remove the infant from his mother immediately after birth, wash him and put him in a cot; only after a period of separation would the baby then be brought to her for feeding and then taken away again. Thus the baby's intra-uterine adaptation to aquatic life is rudely interrupted, not only by birth but also by custom. The protective skin substances are removed by washing and the relation to his mother broken just when a more empathic understanding of the baby would feel it to be undesirable.

Infant feeding is likewise controlled to a large extent by custom. Regular feeding techniques, regular potting and methods of habit training have been based on custom rather than knowledge of the kind of handling that an infant needs, and other examples could be multiplied from everyday experience.

Their significance cannot, however, be easily grasped because they are commonly accepted without much or any reflection and are too near at hand to be seen in perspective. Studies made of primitive tribes by social anthropologists show more easily, because they are less imminent and less laden with potential affect, how the customs of infant management relate to the culture in which the infant will one day live. The studies are made in relatively small societies and are easier to envisage than the large western ones which in any case comprise a variety of differing sub-cultures.

Comparative studies show clearly that radically different customs can be successful. By contrast with ours, other cultures have come to give far greater importance to a father's usefulness, in that he may participate in birth. Turning to the baby, infants may first be suckled by a 'wet nurse' because the colostrum is conceived to be bad for them; alternatively mother may take sole charge and feed her baby not for the short period current in our society, but for up to three years. During this period the husband can be partly excluded as a sexual partner, for his wife is expected to devote all her libido to her infant.

A prominent feature of all these researches is that varying methods of infant care are intimately related to behaviour that will be required of the child, adolescent and adult in society.

Applying this idea to our culture, the revolutionary change that has today begun to emerge in infant care and the upbringing of children must be socially significant. Indeed, whereas before the mother first and the other adult members of the family were the centre of the scene, today the satisfaction of the infant's developing needs is now becoming more and more central. Concurrently new attitudes and methods of education are being introduced which diminish the importance of discipline and seek to meet the developing needs of children. Sometimes the changes are determined by scientific knowledge, but not often, and it is far more likely that they are part and parcel of the idealisation of democracy. Since this is supposed to require more sense of responsibility from the individual, it is thought desirable to foster it as early as possible. Therefore to ask what does an infant need from his mother so as to develop himself, not how can he be made to conform to specified requirements, acquires extra significance.

The relatively new attitude has not, it is true, arisen from sociological reflections. It has rather derived from investigating the psychopathology of patients and discovering the causes of mental illness. Nonetheless the breadth as well as the depth dimensions from which new ideas and techniques of infant care derive are worthy of consideration. They lead us to realise that, if we know the conditions under which babies, children and adults will remain healthy, application of this knowledge will cut across longstanding cultural behaviour patterns. These need to be changed if any particular mother is to receive sufficient support for her to use such a technique as demand feeding of her baby or for the father to participate in his wife's pregnancy, labour and infant care. In other words it is not only knowledge of infant welfare that is needed even to prevent mental disease, but also personal and social knowledge. For the mental health of an infant necessary changes in attitude that seem revolutionary may be vigorously resisted and can indeed make it impossible to implement what is patently needed in any particular case.

The next complementary question to ask is what capacity has the child – an infant has none – of meeting collective behaviour patterns from within himself? When does he begin to relate directly to the culture pattern, its shadow the collective unconscious, and the stream of history which lies behind each? It is obvious that he is not immersed in them from the start; quite the reverse, he grows towards them, and may only confront them directly at adolescence.

Jung laid particular emphasis on the objective independence of the collective unconscious from the ego. The unconscious, he found, was expressed in forms of creative imagination which take on the character of being objective. At once many children's fantasies and statements spring to mind as analogous. When a child asserts that he has a brother or sister who does not exist in reality, he can develop his fantasy as if it were objective and feel it to be true. He may say during a thunderstorm, 'He's angry', and when a simple rational explanation is given he waits till it is finished and then reasserts, 'There's people up there and he is angry.' Such communications, which adults conceive as subjective or magical thinking, are still experienced by the child as objective because they stem from a level at which the inner subjective source of them is not differentiated from the outer realities. Such occurrences are common in infancy and have been elaborated in the study of early object relations. In Chapter 6 it was shown that the probable age at which the infant can experience his mother and himself as whole persons with any degree of stability is at about seven months. At about that age an infant's personal life begins, and before that time part objects predominate. Then the ego has not developed far enough for a whole person to be represented; there can be no subject and object in the later sense; and there is much experience of their fusion and unity. All experiences in the period before seven months are thus pre-personal and objective, and the unity between and fusion of subject and object is also relevant because in the collective unconscious fusion between individuals is an essential requirement. Without it there would be no collective unconscious and no mass psychology.

It would appear, therefore, that the early origins of impersonal elements which develop into the collective unconscious in later life are to be sought for in this very early period; it is necessary to assume that the pre-personal ruthless part objects persist and develop to create a non-human environment. It is during this early period that transitional objects are formed.

Winnicott held that they form the root of cultural life because they are intermediate between the inner world and the outer world of real objects. He worked out a series of stages in the development of transitional phenomena – they acquire a meaning and texture; they show vitality and have a reality of their own, later they become thoughts, fantasies and, it may be added, dreams, by a process of diffusion. When this has gone far enough the original objects are 'relegated to limbo'. It may therefore be conjectured that transitional phenomena are an ontogenetic root of the 'objective psyche': they are archetypal in nature and so contribute in essential respects to artistic, religious and other spiritual experience. Though this thesis has not been fully worked out data are accumulating from various sources that bear out Winnicott's idea. Some have been provided in the chapter on play (c.f. supra p.13ff.) and the reader may like to speculate on whether the numinous images in the chapter on dreams (supra p.29ff.) and also the cover picture are derivatives of transitional phenomena. Attractive as this vision may be, once again I do not think its generalised form can be substantiated: transitional objects are not sufficiently common in infant and child development.

A volume called *Children and their Religion*, by Lewis (1962), contains much relevant material, and especially the interaction between the child and his religious environment. She studied the objective elements in children's play and fantasy related to religious instruction which could be furthered or obstructed according to the way and time it was given. She also wrote an interesting study on group activity in which she shows how objective fantasy forms a factor that sustains group coherence. The children formed gangs as it were around these symbols whose significance died away as the purpose for which the group seemed to have formed no longer continued to operate.

The persistence of the objective nature of objects is maintained and their development facilitated by periodic regressions. Thus there is a positive place for regression which ensures that ongoing personalising trends do not dissociate the personality from earlier and more primitive modes of response needed for social adaptation.

In early childhood, access to the non-ego is easy, but later on, as the ego becomes stronger and self representations get more firmly established, defence systems are built up and it is only possible to contact them through controlled regression. In periods of crisis, such as occur frequently in infancy, acutely at adolescence and subsequently in the later-life crises studied by Jung, regression is required to maintain continuity of being. In this process a deintegrating–integrating sequence is at the same time reached which creates the conditions for ongoing change.

By considering early infantile psychodynamics it has become possible to understand how parts of the psyche are separated off so as to form a relatively permanent non-ego, composed of impersonal objects, and to understand how they may be made accessible to consciousness when necessary. There is a further state of affairs that needs assessment. During maturation the infant's anxiety about his aggressive drives is especially significant. Aggressive objects tend to be excluded from the main body of the self because of the need to form self representations in the infant that are felt to be good. The bad objects are not only extruded but also shut out of the self-integrate. These projected bad objects, at first felt as parts of the child's own or his mother's body, are progressively displaced into a non-human object. That this mode of managing bad objects may be common is supported by infant observation, reconstructions, and by the early dreams of children. It is probably the close relation of pre-personal and later impersonal forms to aggressive and destructive drives that has given rise to the belief that the archetypal contents are dangerous for children. As has been seen (Chapter 3), anxiety dreams of animals biting and attacking the small child are common. Furthermore, early on, non-personal representations have been recorded in dreams, particularly fire and water.

In Jung's conception, however, the collective unconscious contains not only dangerous destructive components, but also good and potentially creative ones as well. Is there then a known mechanism by which good objects can be extruded and kept separate from the individuating process in infancy? The answer is easy to give: good objects are idealised and kept separate from the personal self representation when the internal world is felt to be overwhelmingly dangerous, and when destructive processes seem to be threatening the infant's good objects. To protect them they are projected into the mother, idealised, made omnipotent and so preserved. As will be seen later, the dreams of small children reflect this state of affairs, for in them their mothers, with very few exceptions, only take on a positive and helpful role in complete dissidence with reality.

By studying schizophrenic disorders of children the most interesting information can be collected about the persistence of very early idealising, pre-personal, projective and introjective processes. By the time these children come for analysis the early states have been considerably modified by maturation processes distorted by very early traumatic situations. The fantasies constructed by these children do not therefore give direct information about infancy itself, but studied in connection with the history of the child's development they give clear indications of when the arrest in maturation started and what in their behaviour derives from them. Especially significant here is the proliferation of non-personal self representations that could easily give rise to the idea that the collective unconscious in childhood is unfathomable, or unbounded.

A schizophrenic boy, named Alan, six years of age, knew the ordinary adult meaning and uses of water, i.e. for washing, drinking, etc., but water also represented babies' urine felt by babies to make floods; this was like rain that was God urinating. The urine could be good, be drunk and do good, or it could be evil and full of poisonous germs which kill you. So God could be good or bad. Inasmuch as water and urine could make a flood, it could drown and kill him and his parents. On the other hand because of this property it was dangerous to him inside and in emotional crises it would be released as urinary incontinence. God flooded the world, like the babies imagined they could drown mummy, and so, as he could feel like a baby, God was inside him as well as outside.

He used the water to make the biggest sea in the world – 'bigger than the Thames or the Atlantic Ocean'; numerous fantasies were enacted on it. It was soft and plastic, so it was mother that he caressed and stroked; it was mother's milk, he drank and it became an ocean inside him; he sucked in the water-breast so that inside him was what he called a 'minnick breast' which could feed unlimited numbers of babies and restore damaged parents. But it was also father's milk which was in his genital, which created babies, and which was sucked or ejected into his mother and into himself to feed and give pleasure. When he felt that his destructiveness had created a desert inside mother, father or himself, then water would redeem the situation as rain or as a river (of tears). Again water in a sink would represent the insides of people and have objects swimming about in it; they could jump in and out, and above all could be seen.

All these meanings for water were expressed verbally by him and were accompanied by suitable activities using water pistols, toys, a sink and a sand tray full of water. It would be difficult anyway, and nearly impossible, to convey in a short space the mixture of creative ingenuity and direct naive simplicity that produced Alan's play and fantasy. The range of affect combined with a mixture of symbolic metaphor and logical thought to make it very impressive to watch and hear it evolving step by step; not in the way I have linked the essential themes together for exposition, but in the context of his relation to his brothers (one of whom was a baby), his parents, Sunday school – where he listened with care and once created a disturbance by contesting the doctrine that God was good – and myself. In spite of its impressiveness the proliferation of imagery was essentially defensive against intense anxieties. Detailed analysis of it led to the roots of the splitting and defensively reconstructive processes, to the very early traumatic situation between his mother and himself as an infant, and to the primal scene which took on terrifying proportions.

As the result of this analysis of the child, the fantasy became manageable and he changed from being absolutely ruthless to showing concern for others, and to an increase in symbolisation with an ability to use his good intellectual capacities.

This example is chosen for another reason besides indicating how collective impersonal imagery develops under the stress of ruthless drives; it also links on to Jung's researches into alchemy. Water is an image used extensively by the alchemists as a symbol of the *materia prima* and of the stone which Jung's penetrating analysis has shown to be a symbol of the self. Is it going too far to suggest that if this boy had grown up in the period of the flowering of alchemy and had come in contact with alchemists, he might have become an alchemist? Naturally he would have needed to recover sufficiently from his infantile schizophrenia first. This is not at all outside the bounds of possibility and actually occurred with analytic help.

One feature in this child's change was that the proliferated imagery from being compulsive and concrete became manageable and symbolic. The change was gradual and depended upon the understanding and management of predominantly destructive drives, and relating his fantasies to the objects and situations from which they were derived.

Much attention has been given to this change, which is known amongst analytical psychologists as the change from concretisation to symbolisation in the formation of collective archetypal and self representations. In Chapter 6 it was postulated that true symbolisation was reached in the deintegrating–integrating sequence called by Klein the depressive position, and in Chapter 10 more attention will be given to this topic.

9 Analytical Psychotherapy

THE ANALYTIC METHOD

Analysis means elucidating complex structures and reducing them into their simpler, ultimately irreducible components. In practice it means listening to and observing a patient so as to find out what complex structures are causing anxiety and need intervention to relieve distress or, if this is not possible, at least to make sense of it.

Interventions by the analyst may be of several kinds. First and foremost he aims to elucidate the situation in the here and now; but because much of what is made clear does not apply to the present situation, i.e. it is transferred from another one, it is necessary to explain what is going on. The data are then interpreted in the light of their origins in the present family situation, in the past, or in the inner world.

To be effective analytic procedures must be used with concern for the patient: the timing and grading of the insights provided is therefore important and an analytical therapist needs to use sympathy and tact as well as his knowledge in all that he does.

In the process of making analytic interpretations synthetic processes are of necessity also involved. Linking unconscious with conscious elements means modifying defences so that different and beneficial new combinations can take place. When this happens the analyst will be led to show his patient what has happened and intervene verbally in this and other ways that are not analytic. Because more than analysis goes on in any treatment the term analytical psychotherapy is more appropriate than 'analysis' pure and simple.

Jung classified his treatment techniques into analytic-reductive and synthetic. Objection can be taken to this division on the grounds that each process goes on in the patient anyway, thus overlooking the fact that a technique represents only the attitude and method of the therapist towards the patient's material.

In child therapy the analytic attitude is most suitable because synthetic processes are very active. There are: first, satisfactions in developing new skills, emotional and physical; second, the overriding urge to grow up based on small physical stature and the real and imagined pleasures that grown-ups enjoy by reason of their size; third, the unconscious maturation processes themselves. For all these reasons it is better to aim at elucidating analysis and providing conditions for the synthetic processes to come into operation on their own as far as the child himself is concerned.

Transference

The most important and therapeutically valuable event is the development of a transference in which projections are made by a patient on to the analytical therapist. The projections create a dynamic situation and ensure that analysis becomes an affective as well as an intellectual procedure.

Because of the transference it is necessary for an analytical psychotherapist himself to have submitted to a training analysis so that he may be able to empathise more easily with his patient. But there is also another reason for including analysis in the training of analytical psychotherapists. The transference projection from the patient tends to evoke a counter-projection, suitably termed counter-transference, which was at first seen in a negative light. It was indeed a frequent source of misrepresentation and mismanagement of patients in the early years of psychotherapeutic practice. A training analysis is the best method of making the counter-transference manageable and of converting it into a useful indicator of the patient's transference, which recent research has shown that it can become in the hands of a skilled practitioner.

There has been much discussion about the relation between counter-transference and empathy, which on occasions are difficult to distinguish, particularly with regressed patients who may not be capable of analysis at all and who need something more akin to primary maternal preoccupation from their analysts. Then analysis becomes secondary to care of the child. To enter into this difficult subject, which is still in need of clarification, does not come within the scope of this chapter. However, the case of Billy, described later, illustrates how physical care can be required during regression even though interpretative methods continue to be useful.

SPECIAL TECHNIQUES OF CHILD THERAPY

This introductory outline suggests that the core of analytical psychotherapy applies to adults or children, but there are special techniques of child therapy which need consideration. They derive from the size of the child, his inability to produce verbal associations, and his dependence upon his parents.

1. A child is brought to a clinic or consulting-room by his parents and so it might be that he is not a willing participant in the undertaking. Indeed this can present serious difficulties, especially when a child's hostility to his analyst is being worked on. But except for special situations his being brought is an expression of his inability to transport himself.

2. Next the symptoms of which his parents complain are not necessarily the same as the ones for which a child feels he needs help. A child in an intense conflict with his parents may indeed refuse help altogether – usually this applies in behaviour disorders and delinquency. On the other hand, children develop anxiety like adults and can, like them, wish to be rid of it; this applies to physical pain, depression, and to physical symptoms causing distress; so there is a wide range of symptoms of distress for which a child may clearly want help in the same sense as his parents.

3. A child's distress is closely related to his parents' anxieties, and indeed the cause of them can often be more in them than himself. This situation is essentially a matter of diagnosis and of providing help for the parents who need it. For this reason a child analyst can need to work in conjunction with an adult therapist to whom parents may be referred if their anxieties are too great and they show signs of wanting treatment for themselves.

4. A more important problem arises from a child's diminished ability to make verbal associations, but in their place play serves, in a rather different way, to provide clues to unconscious processes at work. Naturally the treatment room has to be accommodated to give greater freedom of movement.

For all these reasons child analytical psychotherapy is a technique which necessitates special training. The expertise that a child analyst has to acquire centres round: starting therapy, since this involves making a family diagnosis; the use of play techniques and the continuing need to look for times when parents need help.

Starting therapy: preliminary diagnosis

When a child is brought to a clinic or consulting-room he usually has some idea why, though he may not have been told about it, and so the child's idea about the interview may be differently expressed or at variance with that of his parents. Having ascertained from his parents the immediate reason for their child's referral, the child can usually be seen on his own once or twice so that when the problem is discussed with his parents the analyst has gained his own impression of the child and gained some indication of his motivation. Sometimes the child will not come into the therapy room on his own and this has to be allowed, at the start anyway.

After these interviews the mother or both parents are interviewed. They may be seen one or more times, indeed as often as seems necessary. These interviews are designed to give what information the parent needs to convey and as much as the analyst needs to know starting from the knowledge he has gained from his meetings with the child. But there is another more important consideration: the degree of transference that the parents bring to the treatment and the degree to which a treatment alliance is likely to develop. It is important that the analyst convey that his or her function is not to interfere with family life and that he or she will listen to the views of parents. For this reason it needs to be made clear that communication needs to be kept up and the analyst will make himself available by the use of the telephone as seems necessary. It is also a good idea if more regular meetings are arranged when the analyst takes holidays. In this way the child analyst takes total responsibility for the treatment – I do not think that parents should be sent automatically for extra help to another therapist.

In these preliminary interviews some important negative information will have been gained. It is for instance fruitless to suggest treating a child unless it is clear that the parents are sufficiently ready and willing to accept and co-operate in the treatment. Often they are not motivated for therapy and this can become apparent at the first interview, when they make clear their wish to obtain help in managing their child. Whilst this situation maintains, any treatment for the child himself has to be approached with great care, for it is extremely important not to undermine parents' feeling of responsibility for their child. Only when they have reached the end of their capacity as parents in particular respects and have decided that their child requires help that they cannot give is the way to analytic treatment open. In such cases they may have worked this out with the child, and so his need for help has become conscious before the interview begins. This situation is not as rare as might be expected, and is best illustrated by parents who have themselves been analysed.

Another situation arises when parents bring their children along because they are near understanding that they want help with their own personal or interpersonal conflicts. The child has become the vehicle for them and consequently therapy for him is not indicated – all he needs is to get his parents off his back so that they do not make him into a scapegoat for their own anxieties.

Leaving on one side the grossly deteriorated family situations when there is nothing to do but remove the child from the home altogether, these are the main diagnostic problems whose implications need to be worked on first.

Diagnosis of the child's condition

Concurrently with understanding the family situation goes investigating the child's state and its relation to his parents' management of it. In this the diagnostic classifications of child psychiatry are useful but insufficient. To decide that a child is autistic, schizophrenic, mentally retarded, hysterical, obsessional, phobic, suffering from an anxiety state or from a behaviour disorder, indicates that the conflict situation has got built into the self. To understand its significance it is necessary to know the origins and structure of the disorder. Observation and history-taking are often, but not always, revealing, and to penetrate further it may be necessary to manage the anxieties of the parents: a diagnosis cannot be arrived at without initiating a therapeutic alliance between therapist, child and parents. Therefore interpretations and other interventions are useful from the beginning, because therapy and diagnosis cannot be completely separated. In a sense, indeed, details of diagnosis are not obtained till the end of analytical psychotherapy.

Nevertheless good indications of where the source of conflict lies can be elicited early on. Here the concept of the actual situation is useful. It is not enough to discover that crisis situations have arisen in the past; it also needs to be decided whether they are active in the present or no. The term 'actual present' used by Jung (c.f. C.W.4, p.166f.) refers to this amalgam of present and past, and also to possibilities for change in the future. To illustrate what is meant: suppose a gifted child is in a regressed state because of traumatic situations in his early life, and suppose his mother is not good with small children and babies, but can relate to a child who can communicate verbally or can play with toys and imagine ingeniously. If her child can, with analytic help, develop out of his regression, then an ongoing relationship can be established and the prospects for the future are good. The actual present here contains a disturbed child whose trauma can be treated, and a mother who can adapt to a healthy child of his age.

Management of parent–child pathology

The situation just described is a favourable one. There has been a traumatic situation earlier in the child's life – it may have been an illness at an unfortunate time when family conflicts were destructive – but his parents will be ready to accept him when he has worked through a situation that no longer maintains. But there are less simple causes for disorders in maturation, and particularly those in which the traumatic condition is not located in time but is continuous because of persisting attitudes in parents operating in the present. Whilst it is possible for a child to influence his parents or behave so differently that he no longer focuses their psychopathology, and whilst parents sometimes change through the transference that they make to the therapist when their child is being treated, neither can be relied upon. When they do not the child will be unable, or will find it very difficult, to develop because he comes up against the same situations which caused his neurosis in his everyday life. The significance of persisting neuroses in parents varies from child to child, from age-group to age-group, from family to family, but by and large if therapy is not to be slowed down or obstructed in the pre-adolescent period, concurrent change in parents is desirable and sometimes necessary. For this reason a child therapist needs to discover what in the parents' attitude is obstructing maturation and if possible to draw it to their notice and provide help for them as well as the child, when they are able to use it. Many parents get on better and function better if they are not induced to submit to a therapy for which they are not motivated. The fact that a mother is ill, and knows it, may indicate that analysis is desirable for her, but in spite of this she may very well know that her child needs therapy for himself and will not let her need come before his. Not until her child's distress is tangibly met and therapy is begun, or in marginal cases until he has recovered, will she become motivated to get help for herself.

Play techniques

To treat a child a play-room and toys are needed. The play-room should be able to accommodate rough play, water being thrown on the floor and paint on the walls. It should therefore have a waterproof floor and painted walls and ceiling, a couch, chairs and a table (small ones for small children), a rug and a cushion are also provided as ordinary familiar furniture. So as to keep the relation personal, the analytical therapist needs to keep toys in a box which can be locked so that the child can keep it clearly in view that the toys belong to the therapist and are for his sole use during the sessions.

Whether in analytic treatment or not play is an essential part of a child's life. That has long been known but it was not taken as such a central part in the treatment of children till Melanie Klein used toys and play to initiate the psychoanalysis of children. Later on, Margaret Lowenfeld elaborated a method of understanding children's conflicts by assembling a large number of toys from which she invited children to choose. She also provided a small sand tray in which the toys could be deployed as the child felt inclined. The result was often illuminating and often displayed archetypal configurations. That fact stimulated a Jungian therapist, Dora Kalff, to use it for therapeutic purposes when sometimes as many as a hundred or so toys were made available. This fascinated a large number of Jungian therapists all over the world and did much to bring them to consider child therapy seriously.

I myself, for a period, adopted the use of a sand tray and many toys but eventually discarded them. My reasons for doing so were as follows: though I thought the method could be therapeutic, as adequate provision of toys is anyway, I found that to display so many of them was liable to cause confusion and did not help work on transference manifestations. Then children from affluent families were familiar with possessing many toys, most of which they had long discarded. Only those which had significance for them for a longer or shorter time were used, so there was no point in presenting them with many. (It is rather important to ascertain which are currently of interest.) Children from less affluent families may be over-impressed by the number and this can diminish their own creative use. The next disadvantage is that if water is available it may be mixed with sand and thrown about the room, making a mess.

It is of interest that Lowenfeld thought the absence of transference to her therapists was due to the sand tray containing libido, which would otherwise go to forming a personal transference. This was also my impression.

It became my practice to provide a basic collection of toys as follows: small toys representing the family – mother, father and sibling; a soft animal or baby; a few wild and domestic animals, and enough fences to make an enclosed space to put them in; a few motor cars or such-like vehicles, and a toy gun; some constructional toys like Lego and some bricks; plasticine or, better, an equivalent which does not adhere too firmly to the furniture or floor; paper, coloured chalks, a pencil and eraser (paints may be added but have the disadvantage that they can be splashed about the room); string and a pair of scissors; water: this may be in a jug or it is better to provide a sink in which the overflow allows for the water to run away faster than it flows from the tap into its container. A small container will be needed and a few boats, though floating objects like bricks will serve.

This list is to some extent personal and may be varied from analyst to analyst.

To this store can be added others for which a particular child has a predilection, or he may bring his own to the session as he feels inclined. In this way the tendency of children to confuse issues in diffuse activity is reduced, this particular defence thrown into relief, and the underlying anxieties more easily brought into the open.

In the course of playing, a child may include the furniture in the room and that may come in for rough handling so that control may have to be exercised. Control may also have to be introduced if the child makes use of the therapist's body, which he may treat lovingly or may attack in potentially destructive ways.

The question of how far the therapist should allow his body to be used is variable. In an earlier part of this book I described a child painting my face and the subsequent use I made of this situation. The account was of such interest that I could not withhold it, but partly through better understanding and partly by not allowing it, such incidents have become rarities. In this context important factors are the kind of clothes worn and the care taken to keep the play-room as clean and attractive-looking as possible.

With suitable play facilities and the preliminary investigations completed it can be assumed that a good enough therapeutic alliance has been established between the analytical therapist, the child and his parents, and that the disorder in the child has been well enough located to warrant proceeding with analytical therapy. Its individual nature makes case description and comment more revealing than further abstract organisation of technical details.

CASE STUDIES

The three case studies which follow are selected because they illustrate complementary aspects of analytical therapy. The first shows just how much a small girl can transform herself given facilitating interviews. The second, Billy, was analytically straightforward and the detailed interviews are designed to show how analysis proceeds and where and why interventions are made or no. Alan, the third example, is a much more abnormal child who illustrates the need for environmental tolerance, holding, and management as well as interpretation. After ending his analysis help was given to his teachers so that the benefits of his treatment could be realised. Environmental therapy could only be given because of the way the ending of analytical therapy took place.

Case 1

A little girl of just over two years was brought to see me because of fits from which she had been suffering for a year previously. In these fits she became completely unconscious. She was lethargic after them and had to be kept in bed for several hours. Apart from this the child hung on to her mother almost all the time and could do none of the usual things for herself which might be expected of a child of two;

she could neither feed nor dress without help. Her elder sister was far more robust and bullied her incessantly.

Administration of luminal resulted in diminishing the fits to about one every week, but did not alter the regression.

At the first interview it was soon clear that the little girl was much too anxious to leave the waiting-room on her own, so I asked her mother to bring her along to the play-room where little could be done with the child, whom I let stand by her mother whilst we discussed the problem. The next time mother and daughter came together as before, but I gave the mother a chair to sit on just outside the door of the play-room. Very timidly the child came into the room; the door was left open. I gave her some chalks and a piece of paper. At first she did not do anything, then she did a slight scribble and to my surprise made a circle, looked up in my direction and said quite distinctly 'me' (meaning herself). Almost at once her whole manner changed and she got down off her chair and played with some toys for several minutes. Then she trotted out of the door back to her mother who confirmed my earlier good impression of her by taking the situation in a natural way so that the child soon came back on her own.

One day, after she was feeling more 'at home', an object fell on the floor and broke. This provoked severe anxiety and she ran back to her mother as before. But she soon returned, and when she did so and had started playing I gave the broken object a name and said, 'mother broken'. This produced an increase in rapport, since I had understood her fear.

I then started making mothers in plasticine and these she broke up. After a time she wanted a baby made. This she tore to pieces in the same way as she had done with the mother. I tried making a father but he was left alone; at no time did she make any destructive attack on the father figure.

At this point I introduced a further remark, and that was to stigmatise the mother and baby as 'naughty'. It increased the activity. I did this in order to reinforce the 'good' part of her and because this was, as it were, her counter-attack against the 'bad' (dark) aspect of the images in question.

Her mother made an interesting observation at this point: she told me that whenever her daughter saw a baby in a perambulator she would have to go and look at it and was not content till she had done so.

Gradually the child wanted the bits and pieces of the

she tried to do this. It annoyed her when the bits of plasticine would not adhere, and she enlisted my help. By now she could stand her mother staying in the waiting-room, and I judged that the essential process for which the child came had been sufficiently worked through, so I suggested dropping the luminal; no fits occurred. In addition, her mother reported a progressive maturation, so that the child, from appearing backward and listless, had become independent, lively and, for her age, extremely competent at handling her own affairs, seeming even precocious. A feature particularly pleasing to the mother was that the child was no longer bullied by her sister, and could co-operate in enjoyable games with her. Five years later I heard from the little girl's mother. Her daughter's development had been most satisfactory and she had started school with pleasure and success.

The discussion of this little girl's play is facilitated if it be divided up as follows:

(a) *The difficulty in separating from her mother*

In my estimation the failure to come with me was not caused by the mother who was not unduly anxious, or embarrassed by the child's anxiety, and further she readily brought her daughter with me to the play-room. The anxiety of the child must therefore have been due to the projection of a terrifying image on to me.

(b) *The event before the destruction of the object*

Of these the most striking was the drawing of a circle and the naming of it. This can be interpreted as a self representation bringing about increase in security and establishing the ego for a brief period. The relief of anxiety can be compared with the tendency to unite with her mother, whose physical presence was needed by the child at this period.

Apparently the necessity for the child is to maintain an image of a whole integrated self which, it would seem, disintegrates easily.

(c) *The breaking of the objects*

The breaking of the object confirmed her worst fears that things and so people go to pieces easily. The tendency to disintegration can lead to the following conclusion. Equation: object=herself=mother. Running back to her mother brings with it necessary reassurance or real stability which can come about in the following ways.

1. It could revive the memory of the whole self image. In support of this it can be said that without memory of a whole mother the little girl could not have gone back to her mother in the crisis of anxiety.

2. It could be that the stability arose because of the reassurance derived from matching the fantasy with reality. If in fantasy her mother was broken up, to find her body whole would bring reassurance that her fantasy about her real mother was not true.

3. The fantasy was very powerful so that the mother had disintegrated and had been made whole again. That was a great achievement.

My naming the broken object as her mother was based upon the identity of object and mother. The naming was possible because of the knowledge that she could be an integrate, a whole child, and that she had distinguished between fantasy and reality.

My activity in making mothers in plasticine – I made them with breasts and named them – was a test to see what she would do. In breaking them up she was acting intentionally towards that which, according to her feeling, had previously happened in psychic reality. Between dismemberment and disintegration there is an essential difference; it is the difference between being torn to pieces and tearing to pieces – the difference between archetypal and ego activity.

Dismemberment in myths is a regular feature of the cults of the Great Mother who is herself the destroyer, the terrible mother who castrates and destroys her son. Through all the differences the same archetypal form reveals itself – the terrible mother upon whom life depends.

The little girl was in the grip of an archetypal experience of dismemberment, and if we are to judge by the good results of working through the event, this must have been one cause of the symptoms, the fits, and the regression the other being its occurrence before enough ego was formed to convert the event into words or fantasy sufficiently.

The concept of deintegration assists in understanding the

child's disorder, for the source of the fits is the dismemberment of the ego by the deintegrating self, a process described as disintegration. This leads to a regression to a level at which the mother herself is in danger when any progression is attempted, particularly when any artificial or imposed attempt to separate mother and child is made. That must have been the original fear of coming to see me. And yet that separation of the ego of the child from the mother is essential if progress is to be made. It all depends on how it happens.

In order to study this problem I have taken separation anxiety as a paradigm of the general problem and studied the effect of not separating mother and child till the child did so herself. This can be carried on until the child exerts her ego and sends her mother away. If the situation be handled thus the essential basis of consciousness is developed, and with it comes increased spontaneity in the form of play. This fits in with the deintegration theory, for the spontaneity of play may be conceived to stem from the deintegration process. It seems to me clear that the most important consideration is that the intention to separate comes from within the child.

The next step taken by the little girl was to ask for a baby to be made, and this she tore to pieces; it is the same dismembering process as that which occurred before but on a different plane. Is it meaningless to the child's play that the rites of dismemberment are associated with fertility? Or can we assume that this child has in herself an archetypal knowledge of the relation between birth and death? But she destroys the baby – it is the next step in consciousness, nearer to the developed myths of Attis and Osiris. Myths contain much more consciousness than is contained in the play and fantasy of little children. There was no younger child in the family; she was the baby – this she knows – and she is now expressing what happened to herself. In doing so some detachment occurs, the baby is no longer herself but another child or baby in the perambulator. Again it is necessary to realise the nature of the whole process represented in her play. The various processes postulated when the fantasy of a disintegrating mother were at their height apply when it happens to the baby. It would seem that she has to go and look either to be sure that the whole baby has not really been destroyed, or to revive the memory of a whole baby, or else to discover that it has been reconstructed.

(d) *The remaking of the objects*
What are the sources of the constructive play initiated by the little girl? Has her mother shown her the desirability of mending broken objects? If so she has applied it to new spheres, since she has played the game of demolishing models of mothers and babies only with me in the transference. Is it guilt that impels her to a constructive effort? If so I was not able to detect any sign of it. It is not, however, necessary to enter into these speculations, for the constructive play follows from the hypothesis already formulated: that seeing her mother intact and seeing the baby whole gave rise to a fantasy of their both having been reconstituted. Somebody had done it, so she would try. At first she could not do it alone, and I had to be that other person; then she could do it without my assistance.

In the little girl's play the process of deintegration can be inferred behind the disintegration. On this hypothesis the pathological process derives from the ego being torn to pieces by the self as it deintegrates and so, instead of a progression in which consciousness grows, a regression results. This regression leads to a level at which an earlier integrate is found based upon the unity of the child. The fits can now be understood as the discharge of the energy which might have gone into a progressive deintegration.

In the play the child worked through the disaster in a modified form and re-established the position of her ego, expressed in growth of a more independent and positive relation to her mother and co-operative play with her sister.

Case 2
[Note: In the following account, comments made after the interviews are inserted in square brackets so as to separate them clearly from the descriptive passages.]

Billy, aged six years and eleven months, was referred because there were difficulties in his relation to his mother: he required excessive tolerance from her because of his aggressive behaviour. Further he was regularly incontinent of faeces and was exhibiting learning difficulties at a school which his mother, probably correctly, thought were due to frequent changes of staff. She was therefore intending to move him to a better school where his elder brother had settled in well.

Billy also showed patently infantile behaviour, especially in wanting to use a baby's bottle to suck from. His mother was ambivalent about his wish but soon after treatment began she allowed him to have the bottle he wanted.

There were features in the child's history relevant to the content of the interviews to be described.

1. Soon after his birth Billy developed an anal abscess which necessitated his being sent into a hospital for several weeks.

2. When he was nine months old his father left his mother. The effect of this was not gone into, but it may be assumed to have affected the mother's attitude towards her baby. Billy's father now lives in France but he visits his children from time to time. He is unrelated to his children's everyday needs and his visits are glamourised with presents and exciting outings.

3. A short time before the referral, Billy's mother had entered hospital to be treated for a dislocated intervertebral disc and her two children had been sent to a good foster-home for children called 'The Ark'. It was at this time that the symptoms became much worse and precipitated the referral to me.

Billy's mother gave a good impression: she seemed warm, resourceful and responsive to her children's needs. Her analyst, with whom I was fortunately able to discuss the case, confirmed my impression, and so Billy's therapy could start right away.

First and second interviews: There had been two interviews before the three to be described in detail. Billy played quite actively and quietly, but he seemed depressed and restless. He made pictures of a dull, murky-coloured house with a large tree beside it. [Though at the time I thought these pictures were self representations (himself in a depressed state) and so expressed his need for help, it was only later that he told me that the house was 'The Ark', where he had been so miserable and where there was no mother to help him. This example illustrates how a child can show his need for help right at the start of the analytic treatment. Knowing his history I could have interpreted his need, but the data he himself offered were insufficient.]

The second time I saw him, and two days before the third interview, I succeeded in making an incomplete interpretation of his anal aggression, and he went home and asked his mother why I mentioned his faeces. His mother tactfully said that it was my way of getting friendly contact with him.

[This acting out was due to the incompleteness of my interpretation which did not link his sense of shame in relation to my knowing about his incontinence.]

Third interview: Billy gave the impression of being rackety and angry. [This behaviour I understood as the consequence of my interpretations at the previous interview.] He was very decided about his wishes and demandingly asked for a pencil which was not amongst his collection of chalks, so I went out of the room and fetched him one. [If a child seems decided about a reasonable demand or if he expresses a wish adapted to reality I fulfil it. On this occasion it was easy to do so, nor would it interfere with the interview; also it facilitated his intention to draw.]

He settled down to make a picture which he constructed as follows: first he made a line across the paper which rose upwards in an incline on the right-hand side. On the top of the 'hill' was a notice with USA on it, which meant 'US Air Force'. Towards the left he carefully constructed a rope ladder, the knots between the cross-bars being carefully made. He became restless after completing several of them and transferred his activity from the incomplete ladder to a tunnel going down into the earth well on the left-hand side of the paper. It soon turned horizontally to the right till it reached a 'cave'. Having completed this part of the drawing, he rather perfunctorily made the ladder link up with the tunnel which was then coloured pale blue, remarking at the same time that there was also a 'red tunnel'. Immediately he vigorously made a red scribble between the rope ladder and the cave, saying that this was 'a man making an explosion'. [This sequence I understood to represent his interest in the inside of his own body and also his mother's (the earth=mother). The man making the explosion was overdetermined. The explosion evidently represented his rage at my interventions. In an interpretation (not recorded) I referred to the violence inside him which produced his incontinence, and this made him angry because in his fantasy I (the man) had done it. The drawing also infers the fantasy of a man inside mother, i.e. the primal scene. It probably also relates to his mother going into hospital and his rage about it. Because of the uncertainty as to which of these meanings was uppermost in his mind I made no detailed interpretation. Considering the situation in retrospect, I might have made one which included my being the man and the explosion of his rage at my, to him, unwarranted intrusion into a private matter – his incontinence – between him and his mother. Because I did not take up this subject there was a shift away from the source of his anxiety.]

Almost immediately there was a change in his manner and he started to draw an aeroplane flying in the air – 'I am good at drawing aeroplanes,' he said. A yellow beam of light was directed forward from the tail and he commented: 'The light is my brother's invention.'

During all this I had been smoking a pipe and he now showed overt interest in it, particularly the smoke. He matched the colour of the exhaust fumes from the tail of the aeroplane with the pipe's smoke.

At this point I suggested that the aeroplane might be going to France and represented his wish to go to see (the searchlight suggested this word) his father. To this he replied at once: 'My father does not come over, he won't send us enough money to go and see him – why won't he? I am saving up money – French money, but I can only get more English money.' [My interpretation produced a more direct and personal communication. That it modified his defensiveness is suggested by his producing more information about his family. I reserved judgement about how far what he said was true.]

I then showed him that the aeroplane represented parts of a person, particularly the exhaust which was the colour of my smoke and smell, and that the exhaust came out from behind the aeroplane like the smells he made with his behind when he pushed out faeces (using the name for them that he used to his mother. I had made it clear to him in an earlier interview that his mother had told me about his encopresis.) [This interpretation includes the child's manifest transference feelings. These had become so evident that it would have been a serious mistake not to have said anything about them. The interpretation was incomplete: I did not press home his interest in my body and its faecal smells (flatus). Here again there were too many possible meanings: as well as representing whole people the aeroplanes were phallic and anal in character. Further there is a defensive element in the play which is evident in the 'flight' away from the aggressive theme.]

He then started on a second aeroplane; it was on the ground and its exhaust was specifically made brown and looked much more like a lump of faeces. [The incomplete interpretation had, it seems, produced a change of feeling.] He then painted out the USA sign. This aeroplane, he said, represented himself. [A reply to and development of my interpretation about the aeroplanes representing people. He has ingested this insight and has used it himself.] Here I made further interpretations, saying I thought he must have been angry with his mother today and had wanted to make explosions inside her (the red scribble) and fly away to his good father whom he had now begun to think I might replace. [This interpretation works on the positive transference and might be thought of as avoiding the negative mood in which he came. However, I thought it undesirable to reverse a positive feeling about me which was clearly developing. There is this danger in interpreting the hostility to his mother: it may lead to his going home feeling that I am an ally against his mother, who will come in for more angry resentment than would otherwise be the case.

The fact that his mother had been in analysis made this interpretation procedure possible, since I knew that she could handle her son's aggression with skill. If this had not been so and if I had not been clear about his mother's capacity for estimating realities as well as her transference to me, I would have been more cautious.]

My intervention released a flood of questions about where I came from, so I told him that I came from London [which he knew] but perhaps he wanted me to come from somewhere else and then I would feel more like his real father.

He then used black paint to fill in and seemingly half smudge out the earth, making some jabbing strokes at the cave, so I told him that he had been angry with his mother because of the cave inside where he came from and where she would not let him climb [the ladder] inside her, so he felt horrid about her. He made a mark in the cave and rapidly drew a line from the cave out of the earth, over the top of the aeroplane and going in the same direction: 'I am off to France,' he remarked. [There is increase in directly expressed sadism, horrid feelings being the evidence of anxiety about it.]

He now finished the picture by drawing a third aeroplane which represented his brother and then he started kicking a ball about the room in an aggressive, self-assertive way.

It was getting on for the end of the interview and I started putting the chalks back in his toy tray. [A useful way of ending the interview is to start putting the toys away. This introduces the end and gives time for the child to give indications of what he feels about it.] He had not played with the toys but now he picked out a white car and a lorry and tried to attach one on to the other. Next he took a detachable ear off an elephant and so I told him he was at once being angry with me for ending the interview and also expressing his wish to stay with me. [A useful opportunity to introduce his ambivalent transference.]

He ended co-operatively by putting his toys away in the cupboard, asking about the key which locked it up and what it was for. I explained, and he locked up the door and went off apparently satisfied. [This interview shows that it is his aggressive fantasies that cause most anxiety. In view of the depression that he felt in 'The Ark' it may safely be assumed that his mother's absence was felt to be related to it.]

Fourth interview: Billy and his mother were sitting together in the waiting-room, which is an open space. On one side are doors into interviewing rooms, and two lavatories. I came out of my room, which was down a passage. It was necessary for me to go past him to go into the lavatory before seeing him. As I came into view he leaped up eagerly and came towards me, anticipating my taking him with me into the play-room. I rejected him, saying, 'I won't be a minute,' and he returned disappointed to his chair. When I returned he was still keen to come with me but the initial enthusiasm was gone. He was dressed in a red coat with Chinese emblems on it. I commented that it looked Chinese and he said that it was his 'happy coat', his 'magic coat'. [There is clearly an increase in his positive transference. The arrangement of the lavatories was unfortunate but in view of the child's encopresis it seemed to me relevant to consider whether I was not showing a counter-transference which needed care. Why should I not be able to contain my faeces?]

Painting began with dark grey clouds, the colour of my pipe smoke on which he had commented before. The colour had appeared before in connection with his aggression; it also suggested, since he had looked bemusedly at my pipe, envy and sadness; his father, he said in reply to my enquiry, smoked cigarettes. I told him that I thought: besides his pleasure at seeing me he felt sad; perhaps in coming to see me he was missing something at home and he had also been disappointed when I went to the lavatory. He replied that his brother had gone swimming but then added that he himself had a cold and it was not good for his cold [to go swimming]. [These observations were crucial to my conduct of the case. In the previous interview there had been evidence of splitting in a pre-ambivalent way. He showed a tendency to idealise me and also his father, and to treat his mother as a bad mother. At the end of the interview there had been evidence of ambivalence – anger at going and a wish to stay combined with ability to separate without anxiety. There were very early traumata, the most important being, in all probability, the disturbance in his relation with his mother owing to his father's breaking up the family; less important, the anal fissure, for which hospitalisation had been necessary, but his combination implies much splitting in the ego and a fixation point at a pre-personal level. However, his achievement of sadness strongly indicated that these very early traumata have not prevented the development of personal self representations or the capacity to symbolise, and also, therefore, that his symptoms could be due to hysterical conversion and his 'depression' not a true depression but the distress and misery of a relatively healthy child who has achieved the depressive position.] He then returned to the painting and started putting in the sky, and the mixed colours made the sky dark. He looked at it, cleared up the blue paint in the paint-box and continued painting. He made the sky blue, remarking at the same time that he would make a rainbow. He also tried cleaning up the white paint and made the clouds brighter. During this period he said that God made the rainbow that he was going to make, a reference to the biblical story of Noah.

[The various factors which made the biblical story appeal to him are particularly clear. They may be summarised as follows:

1. The name of the home he went to was 'The Ark'.

2. The destructive rage of God corresponded to his own rage at his mother's absence and the way his father 'neglected' him (c.f. also infra for his omnipotent transference fantasy of drowning me).

3. He, like God, feels sorry for what he has done (in his fantasy).

4. And all is made happy again, reparation motivated by sadness and guilt.]

There was an area left on the right-top corner of the painting. The sun was going to be there and he made great efforts to get the yellow paint clean but without success because the paint was dirty. I commented on this and he went over to the sink to change the water. He emptied the dirty water away and then noticed that there was a water pistol, which he filled and squirted on to the floor with an excited look at me. I did nothing because he seemed to be testing me and wondering what I would do. Before returning to his painting he emptied a considerable amount of the water out of the jar on to the floor and returned triumphantly to continue his painting. The yellow paint was easily cleaned up and the sun was put in – a good bright shining yellow object. There was a running verbal interchange going on between us all this time, but not interpretative.

He then started on the rainbow: yellow at the top, then a mixed colour (green), an impure red was followed by a brown, and then a line of black followed by a clear blue one. Yellow and blue were the 'happy' colours, he said, so the rainbow represents a change in feeling, first an excited happy feeling then a change towards sadness, and I got the impression that the black line was put in to remind him of a feeling that was not so much there now as one that he had started with; the ending was a happy blue.

At this point I interpreted that when he poured the water on the floor he had shown his angry wish to drown me and how he had felt like God – because he could do as he wished – who drowned the world and felt sorry about it afterwards. To this he gave delighted assent and made a black top to a house. He changed his technique after this and looked in the box of chalks where he had put the pencil. At first he thought it was not there but with relief he found it and used it to make the vertical walls of the house and painted windows, door and walls in yellow and green.

I then interpreted that the black was his black feelings about his mother and the house was now happy since his anger had changed into happiness that his mother and I had not been drowned. At this he expressed his pleasure by movements and his affirmation of what I had said was underlined by adding a bright red chimney and bright blue smoke coming out. His mother and he were next painted in together on the left side of the house. The figures were rapidly done without minding about the colours much. On the other side was his brother's 'big head'. He made a large head and laid great emphasis on the smallness of his brother's body. The green earth was painted at the bottom of the paper.

The picture completed, he lay back in the chair with his legs apart and half flexed. He turned his attention to me. Where did I come from, he persisted again, and I told him that he knew I came from London but that he wished I came from France like his father. He continued: 'Why don't you come and live with us?' I said that I had a house of my own, but he persisted, 'Why don't you put your house inside mine?' [I left this wish without comment. Here again there is much over-determination.

1. There is a wish for his parents to be united again since I represented his father.

2. There is a personal, passive, homosexual element.

3. There is a fusion wish of a complex kind in which there is an identification with his mother and behind that an oral feeding need in which I would be representing the breast, and his house his own body with an entrance – his mouth.]

It was getting on towards time and I said that I would collect up the toys and put them away. He helped in this after some resistance and carried the toys out himself. The key to the cupboard had a label on it on which 'Dr Fordham' was written. 'Why', he said, 'are you called "Dr Fordham"? My father is called *Mr* X and not *Dr* X. I don't need a doctor, I'm not ill,' and he went off reflectively back to his mother. [The identification of me with his father is rejected.]

Fifth interview: The next time he came to see me, two days later, he felt ill and had also been sick on the way. His mother explained to me that they had not returned home because she thought it might be 'worry sickness'. I took him into the play-room; his skin was cold and his pulse weak so I settled him down on the couch with a rug over him, fetched a glass of milk which he said he would like and put it beside him. [The vomiting was, as subsequent events showed, probably a conversion symptom. But assuming that there is a need for regression, because of his early history, it is justifiable to treat him as if he were an infant. Besides this there were clear indications of physical shock.]

I made interpretations about how, as he came in the car, he felt bad, angry feelings about me inside him which felt like bad food. He soon began to move about and a lot of regressive movements began, curling up, imagining he was being inside his mother, sucking his thumb, etc. Gradually the colour returned to his face and by the end of the interview he had recovered, saying he was glad that the milk had been there though he did not want [to drink] it.

During this interview I pointed out to him that this time he wanted me to be a doctor, then he could feel that he was a patient and that he had really felt he wanted help with his bad insides [a reference to his faecal incontinence and his sickness.

This interview illustrates how the need for care during a regression took precedence over intepretative insights, which were, however, used and provided a valuable adjunct to the child's dependent need for care.]

Case 3

For most children, and Billy was one of them, the impact of their conflicts is on the family. But they can spread over to school and are then liable to penetrate into the collective shadow. Help which teachers may need quite acutely cannot be provided easily because they do not ask for it for themselves but for their management of an often very difficult child. The following case illustrates how collaboration can be achieved during, and can make an active contribution to the successful outcome of, analytical therapy.

The kind of social problems which arise are thrown most clearly into relief by children who are most abnormal, and particularly those who excite the collective unconscious by the ruthlessness of their affects. These are the schizoid, schizophrenic or autistic children who tend to fascinate, repel or horrify those who come across them. Alan was such a boy.

He was seven years old when I first saw him and his relation to others was seriously disturbed. Indeed his mother found him largely inaccessible to her care and nobody else could do much better.

Some years before he was referred to me, his parents had been advised to send him to a special school because his capacity to be educated seemed virtually nil. They refused to do this and decided to try to get Alan well on their own. He improved somewhat and they were fortunate in finding a school with a teacher who was especially tolerant – more of this later.

It was clear when Alan first came to see me with his parents that he was aware of his illness and wanted the kind of help which he imagined I could give him. At the first interview analytic work started, and this continued till the end.

During his analysis Alan developed increasing control over his fantasies and his sexual and destructive impulses. He became affectionate with his mother, more tolerant and understanding of his two younger brothers, and accepted necessary discipline from both parents. The external changes corresponded with changes within the transference where he worked out in detail his terrifying omnipotent fantasies and impulses. The decrease in omnipotence was reflected in the form of his play. What were first gods and devils ended up as cowboys and Indians.

Since he showed so much improvement I felt I could consider ending the analysis when Alan's parents felt more and more they wanted and were able to take responsibility for their child. Before a holiday break Alan had regressed somewhat to more violent fantasies, but when away he sent me a postcard, without prompting from his parents, saying what a good holiday he was having, giving illustrations. When he came back I told him that I thought that since he could now be happy with his family when I was not there, we might consider stopping his interviews. There was no direct response; instead, he started a game he had been playing before his holiday – animals were threatened by men or devils who were smoke. Mysteriously the animals kept getting killed – eleven were reduced to four – and then he started asking how much more time there was. I interpreted that his anxiety about the time meant that he wanted to be sure I would control the devils if he could not. His game continued: the animals were reduced to one, but this one conquered the devils, and brought the dead animals back to life. Alan asserted as this happened: 'So the good powers overcame the evil.'

His play showed regressive features as compared with its

contents before the holiday break. Evidently it had been precipitated by my introducing the subject of ending his interviews. This was to be expected because of the anxiety that stopping precipitated. In the next interview the destruction was much less, and when I said that I did not seem necessary to him in controlling his feelings, he looked pleased and proud of himself. I then told him that the next time would be the last.

In his last interview he was more friendly and open than before, and there was less destruction. It finished as follows: when I announced the end, he got behind a chair, and the excited look came into his eyes which once went with turning over the furniture violently. After an internal struggle, he jumped on the table and the interview ended with my carrying him out on my shoulders along the passage to his mother, with whom he went off down the stairs. The end was excited; there was little sign of regret, mainly fury and rage which he controlled in a way that I can only describe as heroic – it was a triumphant, omnipotent exit. The point to emphasise is that before this, though he had regressed, he had controlled his regression with minimal help and there had been minimal triumph.

In this short account I have tried to convey why I was sure he could adapt himself well enough if given the chance. The certainty stemmed not only from the final episode but from numerous earlier occasions, on which his 'good' self had succeeded not so much in triumphing over, as in standing the impact of, his destructive impulses and their fantasy equivalents. There had been signs of showing concern about his destructiveness, and some reparative wishes, but these were not prominent. From subsequent reports it appears that he had more ability to feel sadness at parting than he had shown openly.

It was after the analytic part of his treatment had ended that the episodes occurred which are especially significant to the present theme. They showed once again, and depended upon, the parents' refusal to let Alan be treated as hopeless. In this they had drawn on manic defence patterns, his father more than his mother, so that it would be difficult for Alan to sustain a development that was more than they had achieved in relation to this father's pathology. It seemed justifiable to expect that Alan would show signs of a defence pattern which was not only socially acceptable but widely approved of.

When the analysis stopped I stated categorically that Alan need not be treated as a special case either at home or at school. It was easy for the parents to implement this idea well enough, but it was made especially effective by two factors.

The first was that Alan's mother had given a great deal of thought, and all the understanding she could, to her son. In doing this she had discovered that, by reflecting on memories of her own childhood and comparing them with Alan's behaviour, she could realise that when she found Alan intolerable it often had to do with herself.

Second, her highly intelligent husband and the paternal grandfather were in many ways like Alan. They both tended to cut themselves off from other people and to make arbitrary decisions relevant to the family. They both suffered from moods and bad tempers. The grandfather in particular had recovered from a 'nervous breakdown'. Alan's father deplored his own faults but was not on the whole intolerant towards them as manifested in his son.

This combination of characteristics made for a home environment that was not too normal for Alan to live in and at the same time was healthy enough. Furthermore, as the result of treatment a significant change occurred in the management of him. If attempts were made to push Alan to behave too well for his capacity, he showed distress signals which both parents had come to understand. Therefore they knew well enough what was beyond his ability to achieve.

Alan's school teachers, however, represented by the headmaster, were not encouraged by hearing that treatment had stopped. They could not appreciate the capacity for normal adaptation that Alan had achieved. To understand why, it will be necessary to consider how this situation had developed.

When Alan first went to the school at the age of five years, he sat at the back of the class and seemed to pay little attention. Soon, however, his class master hit on the rather happy device of giving him permission to wander off into the library during the classes. Alan looked at and later read books and picked up a good deal of haphazard information. This approach led to the teacher's developing a rather unique relation with Alan, which made it difficult for the other masters. Alan took it as his right to behave with all the others as he behaved with his class teacher, and thus he came to hold a special position in the school, enhanced by the fact that he was regularly absent three times a week when he came for analytic treatment.

When the analysis ended the situation at school was better, in that Alan was more friendly towards other children and had even collected a number of them round him, showing promise of becoming a leader; but he did not participate in class work, and his educational attainment was patchy – mostly well below the average.

As Alan grew older and when the hoped-for result from treatment with me had not materialised, the masters' tolerance became strained. Alan's presence in the school became a source of anxiety and the headmaster could scarcely restrain his wish to expel the boy from his school. Alan's father fought hard to keep Alan where he was; he could be very awkward and penetrating in his arguments, but, even with my support, he could not succeed in preventing the demand that Alan be moved to a school for maladjusted children. At this point intervention on my part seemed indicated.

After Alan's analysis stopped, no intervention by the clinic staff was required other than occasional contacts with his parents by interview, telephone or letter. However, Alan became something of a *cause célèbre*, as will be apparent from the numerous people that were involved: Alan himself and his parents; his class teacher; later a special coach; his headmaster; social workers; and the clinic staff, including myself. Therefore, when the conflict reached a sufficient pitch, a conference was held to which all the participants were invited – only Alan being left out.

The discussion centred on the headmaster's anxiety. Fortunately this could be modified sufficiently for him not to expel Alan from his school immediately. It was the group as a whole that did this; my part in it was to draw out the various ideas that were there to be expressed, without giving much expression to my own. When, for instance, Alan's supposed inaccessibility to discipline was made much of, doubts could be sown in the headmaster's mind by asking Alan's father to say what he found, and then starting a discussion about the very different accounts about how Alan responded. Another source of anxiety centred on Alan's intellectual subnormality. It was possible to refer to parts of Alan's achievement which showed promise, but this was inadequate for the headmaster who still could not contain his anxiety. He continued to emphasise Alan's abnormality and to think of him as a blemish on his school.

Then a further crisis arose because his class teacher could not go on giving him special care; he was leaving the school, and Alan would therefore have to go to classes where he would meet other less skilled and tolerant teachers. This necessitated a second conference, and during it the headmaster's argument changed – he feared that with less sensitive methods Alan might be damaged beyond repair. Also, the headmaster did not believe the reports of Alan's intelligence and thought it out of the question for him to pass the eleven-plus (qualifying) examination and to go to a grammar school, as his special teacher claimed was possible.

I was reasonably sure that the earlier intelligence quotients were not a correct estimate of Alan's present ability, and said so, suggesting that this was the time to retest him. The headmaster capitulated and agreed to let Alan stay in his school so long as the test turned out as hoped for and if I would be prepared to treat him further if necessary. I readily agreed, but was sure that therapy would not be necessary. The result of the test was an Intelligence Quotient of 120, with a scatter and some correct answers at superior adult level.

It was less easy to persuade the special teacher to relinquish her relationship with Alan because he fascinated her, but at length she did so. Alan passed his qualifying examination and was admitted to the grammar school where he maintained himself successfully, and there has been no relapse. Indeed, when I last heard of him he was on the staff of a well-known university.

10 Symbol Formation

In this concluding chapter I want to present and discuss a case which illustrates essential arguments in this book. It will also provide an opportunity to go further into the subject of symbol formation, a prominent feature of analytical psychology, to which insufficient attention has so far been given in earlier chapters.

John – an Italian boy aged five years when he came to the clinic – had exhibited states of violent and often manic excitement for about one year before he was seen; in them his sense of reality was so defective that ordinary methods of control, such as restraint and punishment, were not effective away from home; in the end a good nursery school, after many attempts to help him, was compelled to exclude him and refer him for treatment. As a first step before this was begun, he was placed in a small group of children who needed special educational care.

John's mother, a warm-hearted woman, tended to become too permissive in her handling of him because of her guilt at having produced such a child. His father, on the other hand, resented his son's behaviour and, being a mixture of bombast and sentimentality, was ineffectual when he tried to exert control; his punishments were often violently resented. In spite of these defects the home was good, because both parents loved their child and wanted to keep him at home. They proved to be helpful and reliable in bringing John for treatment, and the preliminary assessment was amply confirmed by several years' knowledge of them.

During the first part of his treatment John's behaviour was dominated by ruthless dissociated behaviour; it could be divided up under three headings: aggression, hearing and speech.

Aggression

At first he showed little overt sign of the violence for which he had been excluded from nursery school, though its presence was suggested by his intense anxieties. He could not, for instance, enter my room without his mother and she remained with him during the interview.

Soon his aggression began to reveal itself and a repetitive drama started. A pathetic look of fear would come into his eyes and he stood rooted to the spot transfixed before an apparently innocent object as if he were hallucinated, as indeed I believe he was. Then he would creep towards the object and abandon himself manically to its destruction.

To prevent the excesses of his destructiveness I had to intervene physically, and this led to the aggression being directed on to my body. He was very alarmed when he emptied water over me for the first time and rushed out of the room after he had done it. Only when I interpreted the situation as follows did he return to the play-room: 'There is a good John and a good Dr Fordham who are together, but in the play-room there is a bad John and a bad Dr Fordham who are destroying each other.'

As he became less afraid of what I would do, he started behaving as if he wanted to force his way into my body by attacking it with his head. He held a theory that adults had a special hole down below that he could get into, and he was trying to test whether that was true or false. This idea was also reflected in his play and linked with his anal aggression, which he demonstrated by bending forward and making gestures with his hands to indicate that faeces were shooting out of his anus, saying at the same time that he was exploding 'bombs'. These activities varied and were elaborated from interview to interview within wide limits. An impulse that occurred regularly was to bite various parts of my body; soon it became apparent that my genital organ was the ultimate object of his oral aggression.

Hearing

When he started making pictures I noticed that ears were a prominent feature in them. He always drew them in the same way, which can best be described as follows: they resembled the two cotyledons on a seedling; the two side leaves, corresponding to the ears, were spread out horizontally on a single stem, which would correspond to the head, body and legs of a person who was not pictured. There was no real head, body or legs in a picture which was scarcely more than a diagram suggesting a visual schema, split off from the more integrated parts of his body ego. I took this to mean that the ears did not convey noise into his body and this correlated with his apparent failure to hear what was said to him, and with the negligible notice he took of the noise he made himself.

Speech
At first he hardly spoke at all and only started to talk freely when I was able to interpret his silences, which were most marked early on in the interview. I told him that his words had got separated from his body, like the ears, and perhaps he had left them outside the clinic. He then told me that the words were indeed in the house opposite the clinic; they got put there, though he did not explain how.

These excerpts from John's behaviour show clear features of the pre-personal behaviour characteristic of the first few months. It is ruthless, unintegrated, violent, and the predominating defence is projection. His body image is fragmented or incomplete and his objects have remained objective, i.e. not part of his self feeling, which had not formed because his internal good objects were not sufficient to counterbalance the bad ones – at this stage there was no reparative behaviour, no feeling that he could repair the havoc he created.

THE SYMBOLIC IMAGE

One day he came into the play-room with his mother and planted several pieces of paper down on the table, saying, 'For frighten people'.

In the small school group that he attended he had been unnaturally compliant when the teacher exerted her authority to control him, in very marked contrast to his behaviour at the clinic and to his regular habit of attacking other children when the teacher was absent. Because of his aggression the children teased him and this made him more violent; thus a vicious circle was set up which disrupted his relationships with children in his own age-group. Today when his teacher attempted to control him so as to break the vicious circle, he behaved quite differently from usual, flying into a rage and abusing her; almost at once he became frightened at what would happen next. The teacher, however, remained passive, understanding the importance of the event, and to her surprise the aggression checked itself spontaneously without her intervention; then he picked up paper and pencils and made several pictures, which on his own initiative he brought for me to see. After his first drawing – a horrific face with enormous mouth and horns – he made others but these were less dramatic; as he made them he became calm and by the time he arrived at the clinic he could put the aim of the first creative image into words: 'For frighten people', he said and stumped off. Later he told me that the horns were devil's horns, that the eyes flashed fire, and that the name of the figure was 'Witch-devil'.

I interpreted his behaviour to myself as a statement that he knew he could be dangerous, and that I had been warned of it by him. When I looked more carefully at the picture I noticed that, though he meant to be horrific, the eyes expressed the pathetic look which I had seen in his own on numerous occasions, and when I turned the paper over, I was not altogether surprised to find kisses on the bottom; above them were a number of mandala-like figures and letters of the alphabet, the latter filling the main part of the paper. As he learns at school it seemed likely that the letters were to help restore his broken relation to the teacher, and the kisses were to express love and gratitude to her for not hurting him and for remaining whole and not being damaged.

One emphasised feature of the drawing was the mouth, whose significance had come out clearly before. The ears, now very large, were united with the head for the first time, whilst the convention that he had used to depict them before had now been turned upside down and converted into a nose. The other feature which associated with his earlier behaviour was the horns on the figure's head. These aggressive objects represented the instruments of penetration which he wished to have on his own head when he tried to get inside my body through the hole that he believed to be there. It is further likely that he had fantasies of making such a hole, for in his play he regularly made 'hills' or 'castles' of sand into which he would burrow, scooping out the interior and looking inside for a dangerous object, usually an animal, until the sand superstructure eventually collapsed.

The picture marked a clear-cut stage in his development and numerous changes took place in his behaviour from now on. He started to come into the play-room on his own; he listened to what was said and could be more readily deflected from any particular destructive purpose he had in mind. Further, he developed games which were recognised for the first time as 'pretend': he would *pretend* to frighten me and turn me out of the room, or alternatively he induced me to assert that I was too frightened to let him into the play-room and I was to shut the door against him so as to make the game more real; then he would burst into the room and take possession of it, asserting that I was the bad 'Witch-devil' myself and must in turn be removed to the passage outside from which John had entered. He had discovered that I, and at the same time the fearful archetypal figure, could be influenced, or even controlled, by him.

Another sign of development was revealed later. He brought a 'bomb', a lead tube filled with pastry which his mother had given him, and threw it with an experimental air on to the stone floor, at the same time putting his hands over his ears 'because of the explosion'. Evidently he wanted to stop the noise causing him distress inside his head; this was the first direct indication that noises meant anything to him. Next he developed his experiment as follows. He started shouting and screaming, sometimes holding his hands over his ears and sometimes keeping his ears open. Thus he discovered the difference between noises inside his head and those outside, for if ears are covered, shouts and screams become much more internal.

There are many interesting features in John's development that depended not only on himself but on the behaviour of his parents, his teacher and myself, which facilitated the change. In the present context, however, it is the development of symbolic representation alongside his greater control and integration of affects, and his capacity to express gratitude and concern in simple direct ways, that are of most interest. It is material of this kind, related to an early collective social situation, from which the ideas of this chapter have been developed. That the child showed psychotic characteristics, like the other one whose ideas grew round water, is only to be expected because the persistence of very infantile structures in older children result specifically in these clinical states in which deintegration appears as disintegration.

One object is missing from John's play – it is the breast which would be expected unless he had hallucinated its destruction by the violent mouth. If so, only when his reparative capacities had been discovered would the original object be reached and represented and only then could his improvement be considered stable. Later indeed, as would be expected, another crisis arose presaged by John wandering from home. In his treatment his oral sadism became more and more open until he attacked and bit ruthlessly the clothes on my chest. In this he was imagining – not, I think, hallucinating – an evil breast. Again the concrete pre-symbolic instinctual energy appeared; its object – the breast – was specific, and working the situation through led to consolidating the previous gains.

To conclude this chapter, the symbolic nature of the image needs to be related to the theoretical model, especially as so much importance has been given to symbolic images because of their capacity to express synthetic individuating processes.

The archetypal content of John's picture was evident and the child's name for it, 'Witch-devil', indicated its hermaphroditic nature, of which there were other signs in the mouth and horns. In these combinations alone it expressed the uniting process characteristic of a symbol which clearly took part in holding together and partially transmuting instinctual impulses deriving from the earlier as well as from the present life of the child, at the same time contributing to bring about greater control over them, i.e. to ego growth.

Jung's definition of a symbol implies that it is not in itself representable but is rather the entity whose manifestations can be witnessed in the uniting of psychic elements. The symbol, in this rather particular sense, is essentially related to the self. From this point of view the whole episode at school and the relevant content of John's analysis may be included in any account of the symbol's contents. Since the self lies behind ego development in infancy and childhood, and since John's ego grew, its development must have been the consequence of the self's synthetic activity brought about not only by John himself but also by the special conditions arranged for him in his treatment and his teacher's perceptive tolerance.

John, it will be remembered, had often attacked me with violence before the occasion on which he started to launch his self-terminated attack upon his teacher. Nothing that occurred with me had been as transforming as the events at school; his therapy had indeed been characterised by gradual changes alone. Therefore the two experiences are worth comparison.

1. At school rage was spontaneously inhibited by the child before any bodily contact had been established. This was not so with me, I had to use physical control.

2. The object of his attack was a woman, whereas I am a man, and this must have been important even though some of his behaviour showed that he did not always distinguish between male and female very clearly.

3. Drawing was part of the curriculum at his school. In his analysis it was allowed and drawing materials were available, but John was not making much use of them at this time.

These considerations show that the main similarity is in the child's aggression and the non-aggressive attitude of the adult. Since he was violent first with me and then with his teacher, it may be that my not retaliating violently, as his father did at home, was a necessary preliminary to his outburst with the teacher at school, and that he did not hit partly because violence with his father was more familiar than with his mother. That his teacher, like me, had controlled his activities often, though unlike me she had not been attacked, would seem to be explained by personal factors. In support of this is the observation that in his analysis John's violence was consistently more difficult to control after his father had smacked him.

It will be remembered that in his rages during analysis the child became quasi- or, as I believe, actually hallucinated. Then as the consequence of my restraining intervention he related the hallucinations to parts of my body in such a way that I was compelled to frustrate him.

At first, it must be assumed, the hallucinatory image had been, from time to time, projected into his teacher's body and had frightened him too much for him to get into a rage with her. But gradually my therapeutic work had lessened his fear and a time came when he could test out the effectiveness of his aggressive defence against the fearful image.

A further factor contributing to the change was the passive attitude and sex of the teacher, which made it possible for him to detach the hallucinated and terrifying figure for the first time. This happened not only because of sexual differences but also because John was able to match the hallucinatory content of the image against reality, a process which he had begun in his analysis and which could be continued at school because of the uniting of sexual differences in the image.

drawing it, and in this his ego got brought into closer relation without needing to identify with it defensively. The nature of the figure, which he also used magically, thus preventing the danger which my body had represented before, is interesting enough, but even more so is the fact that he had constructed it. This showed how much his ego had gained in strength and could now not only control his emotion but also allow the reparative processes already described in his second picture, made on the back of the first, to express themselves.

It is the changed attitude of the ego that was most instrumental in altering hallucination and physical violence into imaginative activity, a sign that preconscious ego fragments, originating in the deintegrates of the self, had become more closely related to and partly built into his ego nucleus. A further confirmation of this view is the increased capacity to distinguish consciously between what is internal and external to himself and greater differentiation of his internal world. The latter is shown by the fact that before the picture he only knew that he had 'bombs' inside him; afterwards he knew that there were not only the noises made by bombs, but also shouts and screams which he could keep inside or release into the outside world. The greater range of play activity and the understanding of 'pretend' is further evidence of ego growth if that be needed.

From this it appears there are four interpenetrating stages in consciousness which have been gone through, all related to the same image. First: hallucinations closely related to physical instinctual object relations, which must be classed as *pre-symbolic*. Second: only when this had been recognised, worked through, and interpreted did imaginative activity result and induce the third stage: a uniting symbol which then operated so as to induce the fourth, in which ego fragments were integrated into the child's main ego nucleus.

The adults in John's immediate environment had an essential part to play in this achievement by creating good conditions for the symbol to come into being. But John himself had to develop far enough on his own before the provisions could be made use of and so become effective.

Appendix

OBSERVATIONS AND REFLECTIONS ON PROBLEMS ARISING IN THE ENGLISH EVACUATION SCHEME

During World War Two I was appointed as consultant to a group of hostels for evacuated children in the Midlands of Great Britain. This provided valuable experience which increased my understanding of the self in childhood and depressive concern as a step on the road to individuation.

The British Government's wartime evacuation scheme was voluntary and, though the majority made use of the available facilities, a reasonable number of children remained in the bombed towns going through the experience of serial attack with their parents. As the severity of the attacks varied, the population would ebb and flow; some children returning home during periods of freedom from bombing to be re-evacuated later on when attacks were renewed. In this way the strength and weakness of family ties would often be revealed.

There was abundant evidence of the children's distress at being removed from home and many of them showed direct or indirect evidence of anxiety about the fate of their parents during bombing attacks; but on the whole they stood up to the strain and succeeded in adapting well enough, though we do not know what the remote effects may be. Undoubtedly the return home presented difficulties but they appear to have been overcome with surprising success.

There was abundant goodwill towards evacuees in the reception areas, particularly in the bombing periods. As a whole a remarkable degree of tolerance was shown towards the children's behaviour, even when it was delinquent, though it was not easy for country people to understand the ways of slum children, used to running the streets, whilst town children and parents too often found the country unbearably quiet or dull. At first no special provision was made for problem children but it soon became clear that a fair number did not adapt to any billet which could be found for them. Accordingly special hostels were set up for children who could not find a niche for themselves in any home.

In some areas a psychiatrist was appointed in a consultative capacity to 'advise' about billeting and to supervise the work of the hostel staffs. It was my task to be one of these psychiatrists. The work proved interesting and productive; moreover, the experience provided confirmation in several respects of the thesis contained in this book. For this reason I have thought it worthwhile to add the following short statement about it.

It should be clearly grasped that evacuation presented us with many children on their own, for we could not enlist the serious help of parents whose problems had consequently to be disregarded in our treatment except in so far as they expressed themselves through the children. But so far as we know, the larger number of children who suffered from abnormalities of one sort or another had homes in which it is difficult to imagine that any child could survive emotionally, whilst a fair number were illegitimate or their parents had died in their earliest years; consequently their early life had been disrupted beyond hope of repair.

This does not mean that the importance of parents was overlooked; on the contrary, every effort was made to encourage them to visit their children. If money was not available for this purpose it was provided by the Government. The hostel staff were encouraged to let parents stay in the hostels, and every effort was made through the various social services to persuade parents to write regularly and where contact had been temporarily lost it was, wherever possible, re-established.

In my work I adopted the method of visiting a few hostels regularly and, whenever possible, used to stay the night so as to experience the more intimate life of the hostel. I would play and talk with the children and compare notes about them with the staff. Some children with particular difficulties which they themselves wished to discuss in detail were seen at a clinic, but none of them was analysed.

The children were only seen at a clinic with their own agreement and the agreement of the hostel staff. At first this rule was not made and I had many unproductive interviews owing to the tendency of the children to develop (more easily than those with real homes) an attitude of persecution towards officials or doctors outside their immediate circle. Once, however, the children grasped the reason for their visit and had personal knowledge of what I was like, then the attitude of persecution could be more easily circumvented.

Discussion about the children with the hostel staff had three functions. In the first place they revealed when the children had got beyond the capacity of the staff to tolerate them; these children were moved elsewhere. In the second place they kept the interest of the staff alive in individual children, and lastly they worked out new ways of handling the group.

As an analytical psychologist I was particularly interested to see whether it was possible to provide an environment in which the children could not merely adapt, but could recover the stability which their past experience had destroyed. These experiences were of three kinds: first, the trauma of evacuation; second, the trauma of being billeted and rebilleted on numerous occasions; and lastly, the experience of their home life which was in almost every case grossly inadequate.

But what kind of environment could be provided? By the time I was appointed most hostels were established and I was confronted with the problem of placing children with the right kind of staff available. (With one exception the members of the staff were untrained in handling difficult children.) What knowledge they accumulated they learned piecemeal in the course of their work.

The staff constituted the main factor in the child's surroundings; the environment was therefore not usually specialised. This seeming disadvantage showed, more clearly than would otherwise have been possible, how the personalities of the staff were the overriding consideration, and as they came to learn something about psychology it was abundantly evident that no method could be employed without taking it into serious account.

A major problem was discipline, about which very different views soon became apparent. In the hostels with more discipline there was less open difficulty with the children. Certain children undoubtedly needed what is commonly termed a 'firm hand' in order to keep their inner conflicts at bay; on the other hand, though these children reached a state of stability their relationship to grown-up people and their whole development were less satisfactory than in the so-called 'free hostels' where discipline and punishment were reduced to a bare minimum and where such phenomena as destructiveness, truancy, stealing and sexual acts were treated as symptoms and handled as such.

It was much harder to run a hostel without punishment.

The enormous activity of the children needed far greater resources on the part of the staff to lead it into channels which would not bring disaster in its train.

It soon became clear that certain children who could not tolerate the 'firm hand' with the accompanying discipline needed freedom. But it was also clear that some children could not be handled simply by relaxing discipline. To illustrate this point consider the example of a boy who did not succeed in a free hostel in which the staff were without doubt extremely skilled in keeping the vitality of the children within bounds.

This boy, A, aged twelve years, had become the leader in a group which had virtually driven the staff out of one hostel. The matron, who had up till then been able to handle children, was reduced to impotent rage so that her discipline proved of no avail against their vigorous anti-social activity. This boy was overtly strong, vigorous and healthy, but in reality he was terrified by the consequences of his capacity for violence. He had in the past suffered from rheumatic fever, had been to convalescent homes and was still afraid that his heart would give out because it was a 'bad', diseased one which might eventually cause his death. In other words this boy felt a strong sense of guilt over his behaviour which was, however, repressed and which reappeared in the form of physical, hypochondriacal anxieties.

The problem which presented itself was as follows: could this child's guilt be brought into consciousness and then modified so as to re-establish the coherence of his psyche? A long attempt to do this was made in a free hostel. What happened? His outbursts of violence were tolerated to the maximum possible extent under the circumstances and many crises were overcome. He developed an excellent sense of responsibility, becoming an asset in the hostel in many respects. For example, he started a 'breakages committee' which took note of the damage done to the hostel, and attempted to make this good. But as he got older it became increasingly difficult to manage him – he was not only destructive to the material but he terrorised the other boys in the group. As this destructiveness grew, his guilt came more and more into the open so that he expressed the belief that he was damned and would without doubt go to hell.

Just at this point it became necessary to remove him since the whole life of the hostel was at stake. He was taken to a large hostel run by an ex-naval petty officer with a talent in handling boys in a firm though kindly way. A became well behaved, lost his violent outbursts, was successful at organised games and 'settled down'. The routine and just discipline in the hostel helped him to organise his life on the basis which he had initiated in the free hostel but which he could not sustain there.

Such a case reveals how delusive is the behaviour criterion in judging whether a child is normal or abnormal, whether he is in need of psychological help or no. It was impossible to handle his problem to its end and so re-establish the coherence of his psyche in a free regime. When the repressive forces were relaxed the whole problem came to light in such a way that he represented a critical social problem. As the result of the altered environment the boy could cover over his problem so that crude observation would make it seem as if it were solved, but this crude process has nothing to do with his rehabilitation in a deeper sense.

As a whole, however, there was little doubt that the free type of hostel produced the best results. The children went away from there with a memory of happiness which they will not easily forget and they had almost all developed in a real way. The other hostels performed a useful role in caring for those children who could not stand the freedom or those who did not need it.

By way of contrast to A let us consider a child who was able to develop a very long way in a free hostel.

When B came to the hostel because his home in London could not tolerate him he was a tremendously alive boy of six years – very active, and continually rushing about. He liked to carry a huge stick about eight feet long which he would wave about and poke at various people or objects. On more than one occasion he broke a window. He showed little or no remorse for his misdeeds; he lacked personal feeling; and his responses were crude and animal-like. On some occasions and in the face of quite mild frustration he would fly into violent rages and smash anything within his reach. If you got angry with him he would scream, cry, and cling to you, imploring you to stop. He showed an almost complete lack of social feeling, so that had he been an adult, one could not have resisted the conclusion that he was in a manic state.

One year after his admission he was in the same kind of condition though modified in the following way: he no longer carried his stick but he still behaved as if haunted by a violent energy from which he could not free himself. At one time he was obsessed by fire and would sit for hours in front of one, fascinated, completely lost to the outer world. He would light fires almost anywhere, so that the hostel staff had to be constantly alive to what he was doing, otherwise he would burn the house down.

Then he developed night terrors of 'white things with eyes behind the curtain' and about the same time he became less demanding and more helpful, more loving and obliging. One year and one month after his admission his mother died – this produced tears, some of which represented genuine grief. To our surprise he became very much concerned about the other members of his family, at this time. He wanted to help them, and thinking that they were 'in a rotten place' asked to have them at the hostel.

His suffering made him change in a radical way, so that he got more personal and pleasant. For instance at meals he would say things like 'Please may I have my cup of tea', instead of the crude, demanding 'Where's my cup of tea!' – two ways of expression which illustrated the change.

Two months later he left the hostel for administrative reasons. He had altered from an impersonal phenomenon to a child with real personal feelings. He had begun to trust the hostel matron. This was no small achievement but it took a matron with very great capacity for understanding children, and tremendous love and tolerance for them, to bring this change about. In addition she had considerable psychological understanding and without doubt this was an important factor in bringing about the pleasing development.

Evacuation showed up the fact that children from early years can be confronted with problems needing the utmost experience and understanding on the part of those in charge of them. It brought home the urgent need for greater knowledge of children and for suitable adults, properly trained in child psychology, to undertake both the care and analysis of them.

It will be recollected that I put forward, in a previous chapter, the view that children became so infected by their parents' problems, as the result of their unconsciousness, that the children themselves usually needed analytic assistance before the particular problem which their symptoms presented could be resolved. Taking the experience of evacuated children in hostels as a whole, I never imagined that my previous somewhat uncertain conclusion about child analysis and the need for it would receive such substantial support.

A question which has always concerned me acutely and which is frequently voiced from other quarters comes in at this juncture: do children need analysis or should they rather be treated entirely by indirect means? This question is psychologically relevant because we have to ask: what is the point in putting children back into the unconscious from which they are gradually emerging? We have tried to answer this question in a previous chapter but some more light can be thrown on the matter from the hostel children.

It is clear that case A could not be cured without analysis. On the other hand case B – though he could have developed further than was actually the case – was remarkably better. It would be easy to cite other examples of striking developments, and this may make it seem that a suitable environment alone will provide a solution to many children's problems. I do not, however, consider that such a conclusion is justified.

It is clear that B's conflicts were not relieved and this applied to all the children that I was able to observe over periods of up to three years. I do not mean to suggest that they could be benefited, for some of them were – as far as our present knowledge goes – beyond basic help. But the fact that their problems were not solved in a radical sense does demonstrate that they need further assistance. Therefore, on these grounds they become the legitimate field of analytical research and therapy.

In addition there are general advantages which analytic understanding possesses over any kind of group treatment: first, the changes are more rapid; second, the child receives deeper understanding of his conflicts than is possible in a group, and as the result does not have to go through so many painful experiences virtually alone; third, analysis goes to the root of the problem as nothing else can; fourth, it makes it possible to 'contain' within the analytical room many antisocial activities which consequently are not acted out in the group; lastly it provides us with more detailed understanding of the child and so assists in the handling of him.

As the bombing became less many evacuees returned home and it was possible to send to the hostels children who needed to be away from home for a period.

The following case, C, provided an example through which we can study the relation of child analysis to the effect of hostel life.

This boy went to a hostel where it had been possible to get very good understanding with the matron who readily understood psychological ideas and applied them with great skill. The boy was aged five years when his analysis started. He had been in analysis for one year, being seen twice a week, when he went to the hostel, so that a good deal was known about him. One outstanding feature was the fear of the consequences of his violent feelings which overwhelmed him completely during his analytical interviews, but which he dare not release elsewhere. He was in the hostel for five months where he was left without any other treatment. During that time he made some development in a social sense but went back in others. Then I took him for further analysis.

At first there seemed a considerable change, he was more friendly and co-operative, but this was only skin-deep. It was certainly a change for the better but it did not touch his fundamental conflicts which soon came to the surface in the same state as before.

He remained at the hostel for one year and five months and I should judge that he improved more quickly than he would have done at home. But my conclusion was that the good environment of the hostel could not expect to bring about the solution of the fundamental conflict. The child was abnormal from birth; he was underweight; he was only breastfed for a very short period and during that time his mother said she nearly fainted when she tried to feed him since she was ill. She struggled on for nine to ten weeks, during which time he got little food. Then he caught pneumonia and was given up for dead but he lived. He never recovered from this bad start and when brought to see me he was carried about in a perambulator.

Such a case is a very severe one, but in spite of its severity the child did show clearly from his analysis what I had inferred from external observations; namely, that more than the good environment provided by the hostels is needed.

Notes

These notes supplement references already given in the text. They are intended to introduce, chapter by chapter, books and articles which have influenced conclusions arrived at, or on which I have written elsewhere. No attempt has been made to cover the whole literature on the subjects selected but enough has been given to gain access to it. Reference to the bibliography which follows is made by dates of publication or, in the case of Jung, by citing the volume of the *Collected Works.*

CHAPTER 1: ANTECEDENTS

A good introduction to Jung's work will be found in Fordham, F., 1966.

The ego and the archetypes
Fordham, M. 'Biological theory and the concept of archetypes' in Fordham, M., 1957. Hobson, 1961. Jung, C.W.7; 'The concept of the collective unconscious' in C.W.9, part 1; also other essays to be found in that volume.

Method
Fordham, M. 'Problems of active imagination' in Fordham, M., 1958. Jung, 'The transcendent function' in C.W.8; 'The technique of differentiating the ego from the unconscious', C.W.7; 'Introduction' to C.W.12; 'The practical use of dream analysis' in C.W.16.

Alchemy and Jung's historical ideas
C.W.9, part 2; 11; 12; 13; 14.

Individuation and mysticism
Fordham, M., 1958, 1985a.

CHAPTER 2: PLAY

Gardner, 1937. Greenacre, 1959. Klein, 1955. Lewis, 1962. Winnicott, 'Why children play' in Winnicott, 1964.

CHAPTER 3: DREAMS

Amplification
Jacobi, 'The dream of the bad animal' in Jacobi, 1959.

Dreams of early childhood
Despert, 1949.

Later dreams
Wickes, 1966.

CHAPTER 4: PICTURES

Baynes, 1955. Eng, 1931. Also Fordham, M., undated. Jung, 'Mandala symbolism' in C.W.9, part 1. Kellogg, 1955. Le Barre, undated. Read, 1943.

CHAPTER 5: THE CONCEPTUAL MODEL

Ego psychology and defences
Arlow and Brenner, 1964. Apfelbaum, 1966. Fairbairn, 1952. Freud, A., 1961. Guntrip, 1961. Hartmann, 1958.

The archetypes
Fordham, M., 'Biological theory and the concept of archetypes' in Fordham, M., 1957; 1962; 1965. Hobson, 1961. Segal, 1964, from which access can be gained to the work of Melanie Klein. Spitz, 1959. Piaget, 1951, and also others of his extensive series of monographs.

The self
Fordham, M., 'Origin of the ego in childhood' and 'Some observations on the self and ego in childhood', both in Fordham, M., 1957; 1963; 1965; 1966.

Reconstruction
Fordham, F., 1964. Fordham, M., 1965b. Rubinfine, 1967.

Infant observation
Bick, 1966. Call, 1964. Escalona, 1963. Spitz, 1946; 1957; etc. Winnicott, 'Observation of infants in a set situation' in Winnicott, 1958.

Infantile autism
Bettelheim, 1967. Fordham, M., 1976.

CHAPTER 6: MATURATION

Intra-uterine life and birth
Greenacre, 1945. Spitz, 1965. Verney and Kelly, 1982.

The nursing couple
Winnicott, 'Primary maternal preoccupation' in Winnicott, 1958. Segal, 1964. Bion, 1962.

Transitional object
Winnicott, 1958 and 1967. Coppolillo, 1967. Fordham, M., 1977.

Identity
Erikson, 1963. Jacobson, 1964–65.

Separation–individuation phase
Fordham, M., 1968. Mahler et al., 1975. Joffe and Sandler, 1965.

Oedipal conflict
Literature too extensive to cite specific items. The argument is developed from Freud's work, Jung's modification of it, and also Klein (c.f. Segal, 1964 and Jacobson, 1964–65).

CHAPTER 7: THE FAMILY

Jung, 'Marriage as a psychological relationship,' C.W.17. Wickes, 1966. Winnicott, 1964, part 2: 'The family'.

CHAPTER 8: THE SOCIAL SETTING

Anthropological studies
Boyer, 1964. Erikson, 1963. Layard, 1942. Mead, 1942. Parin and Morgenthaler, 1964.

Adolescence
Henderson, 1967.

CHAPTER 9: ANALYTICAL PSYCHOTHERAPY

Aldridge, 1959. Fordham, M., 1976 and 1985a. Hawkey, 1945; 1951; 1955; 1964. Jung: case studies in 'The Theory of psychoanalysis' in C.W.4; 'Analytical psychology and education' in C.W.17. Kalff, 1962. Case 1 was previously reported in Fordham, M., 1957, p.148ff. Case 3 has been described in more detail in Fordham, M., 1976. Tate, 1958 and 1961. Wickes, 1966.

CHAPTER 10: SYMBOL FORMATION

Fordham, M., 'Reflections on image and symbol' in Fordham, M., 1957. Jackson, 1963. Jung, 'Definition of symbol' in Jung, 1923. Stein, 1957.

BIBLIOGRAPHY

Abraham, K. (1914) 'Review of Jung's *Versuch einer Darestllung der Psycho-analytischen Theorie*' in *Clinical Papers and Essays on Psycho-Analysis*: London, Hogarth, 1955.

Aldridge, M. (1959) 'The birth of the black and white twins', *J. Analyt. Psychol.*, 4, 1.

Apfelbaum, B. (1966) 'On ego psychology: a critique of the structural approach to psycho-analytic theory', *Int. J. Psycho-Anal.*, 47, 4.

Arlow, J.A. and Brenner, C. (1964) *Psychoanalytic Concepts and the Structural Theory*: New York, International Universities Press.

Baynes, H.G. (1936) 'The psychological background of the parent–child relationship' in *Analytical Psychology and the English Mind*: London, Methuen, 1950.

Baynes, H.G. (1955) *Mythology of the Soul*: London, Routledge & Kegan Paul.

Bettelheim, B. (1967) *The Empty Fortress*: New York, Free Press; London, Collier Macmillan.

Bick, E. (1966) 'Notes on infant observation in psycho-analytic training', *Int. J. Psycho-Anal.*, 45, 4.

Bion, W.R. (1962) *Learning from Experience*: London, Heinemann.

Bion, W.R. (1970) 'Attention and interpretation' in *Seven Servants*: New York, Aronson, 1977.

Boyer, L.B. (1964) 'Psychological problems of a group of Apaches: alcoholism, hallucinations and latent homosexuality among typical men', *The Psychoanalytic Study of Society*, 3: New York, International Universities Press.

Call, J.D. (1964) 'Newborn approach behaviour and early ego development', *Int. J. Psycho-Anal.*, 45, 2–3.

Collins, M. (1963) 'The stimulus of Jung's concept in child psychiatry' in *Contact with Jung*, ed. M. Fordham: London, Tavistock.

Coppolillo, H.P. (1967) 'Maturational aspects of the transitional phenomenon', *Int. J. Psycho-Anal.*, 48, 2.

Despert, J.L. (1949) 'Dreams in children of pre-school age', *Psychoanalytic Study of the Child*, 3–4: New York, International Universities Press.

Edinger, E.F. (1960) 'The ego self paradox', *J. Analyt. Psychol.*, 5, 1.

Eng, H. (1931) *The Psychology of Children's Drawings*: London, Kegan Paul.

Erikson, E. (1963) *Childhood and Society*, 2nd edn: New York, Norton.

Escalona, S.K. (1963) 'Patterns of infantile experience and the developmental process', *Psychoanalytic Study of the Child*, 18: New York, International Universities Press.

Fairbairn, W.R.D. (1952) *Psychoanalytic Studies of the Personality*: London, Tavistock; New York, Basic Books.

Fordham, F. (1964) 'The care of regressed patients and the child archetype', *J. Analyt. Psychol.*, 9, 1.

Fordham, F. (1966) *An Introduction to Jung's Psychology*: Harmondsworth, Penguin Books.

Fordham, F. (1963) 'Myths, archetypes and patterns of childhood', *Harvest Journal of the Analytical Psychology Club*, 9.

Fordham, M. (undated) 'The meaning of children's pictures', *Apropos no. 2*: London, Lund Humphries.

Fordham, M. (1957) *New Developments in Analytical Psychology*: London, Routledge & Kegan Paul.

Fordham, M. (1958) *The Objective Psyche*: London, Routledge.

Fordham, M. (1958a) 'Individuation and ego development', *J. Analyt. Psychol.*, 3, 2.

Fordham, M. (1962) 'The theory of archetypes as applied to child development with particular reference to the self' in *The Archetype*, ed. G. Adler: Basel/New York, Klarger.

Fordham, M. (1963) 'The empirical foundation and theories of the self in Jung's works', *J. Analyt. Psychol.*, 8, 1.

Fordham, M. (1963a) 'Notes on the transference and its management in a schizoid child', *J. Child Psychother.*, 1, 1.

Fordham, M. (1964) 'Well motivated parents', *J. Analyt. Psychol.*, 9, 2.

Fordham, M. (1965) 'The self in childhood', *Psychother. Psychosom.*, 13.

Fordham, M. (1965a) 'Review of *The Self and the Object World* by E. Jacobson', *Int. J. Psycho-Anal.*, 46, 4.

Fordham, M. (1965b) 'The importance of analysing childhood for the assimilation of the shadow', *J. Analyt. Psychol.*, 10, 1.

Fordham, M. (1966) 'Review of Harding's *The Parental Image*', *J. Analyt. Psychol.*, 11, 1.

Fordham, M. (1968) 'Individuation in childhood' in *The Reality of the Psyche*, ed. J. Wheelwright: New York, Putnam.

Fordham, M. (1968a) 'Theorie und Praxis der Kinderanalyse aus der Sicht der analytischen Psychologie C.G. Jungs' in *Handbuch der Kinderpsychotherapie*, ed. G. Biermann: Munich/Basel, Reinhardt.

Fordham, M. (1969) 'Technique and countertransference' in *Technique in Jungian Analysis*, eds M. Fordham, R. Gordon, J. Hubback and K. Lambert: London, Heinemann.

Fordham, M. (1971) Maturation of the ego and the self' in *Analytical Psychology a Modern Science*, eds M. Fordham, R. Gordon, J. Hubback, K. Lambert and M. Williams: London, Heinemann.

Fordham, M. (1976) *The Self and Autism*: London, Heinemann.

Fordham, M. (1977) 'A possible root of active imagination' in *Jungian Psychotherapy*: London, Karnac, 1986.

Fordham, M. (1979) 'Analytical psychology and countertransference' in *Countertransference*, eds L. Epstein and A.H. Feiner: New York and London, Aronson.

Fordham, M. (1985) 'Abandonment in infancy' in *Chiron*, eds N. Swartz-Salant and M. Stein: Wilmette, Chiron.

Fordham, M. (1985a) *Explorations into the Self*: London, Academic Press.

Fordham, M. (1985b) 'The self in Jung's works' in Fordham (1985a).

Fordham, M. (1985c) 'Integration–deintegration in infancy' in Fordham (1985a).

Fordham, M. (1986) *Jungian Psychotherapy*: London, Karnac.

Frazer, J.G. (1930) *Myths of the Origin of Fire*: London, Macmillan.

Freud, A. (1961) *The Ego and the Mechanisms of Defence*: London, Hogarth.

Freud, S. (1937) 'Constructions in analysis' in *Collected Papers*, 5: London, Hogarth, 1950.

Gardner, D.E.M. (1937) *The Children's Play Centre*: London, Methuen.

Greenacre, P. (1945) 'The biologic economy of birth', *Psycho-*

analytic Study of the Child, 1: New York, International Universities Press.

Greenacre, P. (1959) 'Play in relation to creative imagination', *Psychoanalytic Study of the Child*, 14: New York, International Universities Press.

Greenberg, M. (1958) *The Birth of a Father*: New York, Continuum.

Guntrip, H. (1961) *Personality Structure and Human Interaction*: London, Hogarth.

Harding, E. (1955) *Woman's Mysteries*: New York, Pantheon.

Harris, M. (1975) *Thinking about Infants and Young Children*: Strath Tay, Clunie Press.

Harrison, J. (1927) *Themis*: Cambridge, Cambridge University Press.

Hartmann, H. (1958) *Ego psychology and the Problem of Adaptation*, trans. D. Rapaport: London, Imago.

Hawkey, L. (1945) 'Play analysis: case study of a nine-year-old child', *Brit. J. Med. Psychol.*, 20, 3.

Hawkey, L. (1951) 'The use of puppets in child psychotherapy', *Brit. J. Med. Psychol.*, 24, 3.

Hawkey, L. (1955) 'The function of the self in adolescence', *Brit. J. Med. Psychol.*, 28, 1.

Hawkey, L. (1962) 'The therapeutic factor in child analysis' in *The Archetype*, ed. G. Adler: Basel/New York, Klarger.

Henderson, J. (1967) *Thresholds of Initiation*: Middletown, Wesleyan University Press.

Hobson, R. (1961) 'Critical notice. C.G. Jung: *Archetypes and the Collective Unconscious*', *J. Analyt Psychol.*, 6, 2.

Hume, R.E., trans. (1931) *The Thirteen Principal Upanishads*: London, Oxford University Press.

Jackson, M. (1963) 'Symbol formation and the delusional transference', *J. Analyt. Psychol.*, 8, 2.

Jacobi, J. (1952) 'Das Kind wird ein Ich', *Heilpädagogische Werkblatter*, 3.

Jacobi, J. (1953) 'Ich und Selbst in der Kinderzeichnung', *Schweiz. Z. Psycholog. anwend.*, 12, 1.

Jacobi, J. (1959) *Complex/Archetype/Symbol in the Psychology of C.G. Jung*: London, Routledge & Kegan Paul.

Jacobi, J. (1967) *The Way of Individuation*: London, Hodder & Stoughton; New York, Harcourt Brace.

Jacobson, E. (1964–65) *The Self and the Object World*: New

York, International Universities Press; London, Hogarth.

Joffe, W.G. and Sandler, J. (1965) 'Notes on pain, depression and individuation' in *Psychoanalytic Study of the Child*, 20: New York, International Universities Press.

Jung, C.G. (1916) *The Psychology of the Unconscious*, trans. B. Hinkle: London, Kegan Paul (revised as C.W.5).

Jung, C.G. (1916a) 'The association method' in *Collected Papers in Analytical Psychology*, ed. C. Long: London, Baillière, Tindall & Cox (parts 1 and 2 in this chapter are published in C.W.2 and part 3 is already available in C.W.17).

Jung, C.G. dir. (1918) *Studies in Word Association*, trans. M.D. Edem: London, Heinemann. (New York, Moffat Yard, 1919).

Jung, C.G. (1923) *Psychological Types*, trans. H.G. Baynes: London, Routledge and Kegan Paul. Revised translation appears as C.W.6.

Jung, C.G. (1957–79) *The Collected Works of C.G. Jung* eds Herbert Read, Michael Fordham and Gerhard Adler; trans. R.F.C. Hull. No. XX in Bollingen Series, Princeton, Princeton University Press; London, Routledge & Kegan Paul. The following volumes are referred to in the text:

2. *Experimental Researches*, 1973
4. *Freud and Psychoanalysis*, 1961
5. *Symbols of Transformation*, 1956
6. *Psychological Types*, 1971
7. *Two Essays on Analytical Psychology*, 2nd edn, 1966
8. *The Structure and Dynamics of the Psyche*, 1960

9, pt 1. *The Archetypes and the Collective Unconscious*, 1968
9, pt 2. *Aion*, 1959

10. *Civilization in Transition*, 2nd edn, 1970
11. *Psychology and Religion: West and East*, 1958
12. *Psychology and Alchemy*, 2nd edn, 1968
13. *Alchemical Studies*, 1967
14. *Mysterium Coniunctionis*, 1963
16. *The Practice of Psychotherapy*, 2nd edn 1966
17. *The Development of Personality*, 1970

Jung, C.G. (1963) *Memories, Dreams, Reflections*: London, Collins and Routledge & Kegan Paul.

Kalff, D.M. (1962) 'Archetypus als heilender Faktor', *The Archetype*, ed. G. Adler: Basel/New York, Klarger.

Keightley, T. (1892) *Fairy Mythology*: London, Bell.

Kellogg, R. (1955) *What Children Scribble and Why*: San Francisco, author's edition.

Klein, M. (1932). *The Psycho-Analysis of Children (The Writings of Melanie Klein, 2):* London, Hogarth, 1980.

Klein, M. (1955) 'The psycho-analytic play technique: its history and significance' in *New Directions in Psycho-Analysis*, eds M. Klein, P. Heimann and R.E. Money-Kyrle: London, Tavistock.

Klein, M. (1955a) 'On identification' in *The Writings of Melanie Klein*, 3: London, Hogarth, 1980.

Klein, M. (1980) *Narrative of a Child Analysis (The Writings of Melanie Klein*, 4): London, Hogarth.

Layard, J. (1942) *Stone Men of Malekula*: London, Chatto & Windus.

Le Barre, H. (undated) *L'enfant et ses dessins*, 2 vols: Pujols (Lot-et-Garonne).

Lewis, E. (1953) 'The function of group play during middle childhood in developing the ego complex', *Brit. J. Med. Psychol.*, 27, 1/2.

Lewis, E. (1962) *Children and their Religion*: London, Sheed & Ward.

Mahler, M., Pine, F. and Bergman, A. (1975) *The Psychological Birth of the Human Infant*: London, Hutchinson.

Marcus, K. (1965) 'Early childhood experiences remembered by adult analysands', *J. Analyt. Psychol.*, 10, 2.

Mead, M. (1942) *Growing up in New Guinea*: London, Penguin Books.

Meltzer, D. and Harris Williams, M. (1988) *The Apprehension of Beauty*: Strath Tay, Clunie Press.

Miller, L., Rustin, M., Rustin, M. and Shuttleworth, J., eds (1989) *Closely Observed Infants*: London, Duckworth.

Moody, R. (1955) 'On the function of the counter-transference', *J. Analyt. Psychol.*, 1, 1.

Moody, R. (1961) 'A contribution to the psychology of the mother–child relationship' in *Current Trends in Analytical Psychology*, ed. G. Adler: London, Tavistock.

Muller, F.M. (1879–84) *Sacred Books of the East*, 15: Oxford, Clarendon Press.

Neumann, E. (1954) *Origins and History of Consciousness*, trans. R.F.C. Hull: London, Routledge & Kegan Paul.

Neumann, E. (1973) *The Child*: London, Hodder & Stoughton.

Parin, P. and Morgenthaler, F. (1964) 'Ego and orality in the analysis of West Africans', *The Psychoanalytic Study of Society*, 3: New York, International Universities Press.

Piaget, J. (1951) *Play, Dreams and Imitation in Childhood*, trans. Gattegno and Hodgson: London/Toronto, Heinemann.

Pine, F. and Furer, M. (1963) 'Studies of the separation–individuation phase: a methodological overview', *Psychoanalytic Study of the Child*, 18: New York, International Universities Press.

Read, H. (1943) *Education through Art*: London, Faber and Faber.

Rosenfeld, H. (1988) *Impasse and Interpretation*: London/New York, Routledge.

Rubinfine, D.L. (1967) 'Notes on the theory of reconstruction', *Brit. J. Med. Psychol.*, 40, 3.

Segal, H. (1964) *Introduction to the Work of Melanie Klein*: London, Heinemann.

Sidoli, M. (1989) *The Unfolding Self*: Boston, Sligo.

Sidoli, M. and Davis, M., eds (1988) *Jungian Child Psychotherapy*: London, Karnac.

Silberer, H. (1917) *Problems of Mysticism and its Symbolism*, trans. S.E. Jelliffe: New York, Moffat Yard.

Spitz, R.A. (1946) 'Anaclitic depression', *Psychoanalytic Study of the Child*, 2: London, Imago.

Spitz, R.A. (1957) *No and Yes*: New York, International Universities Press.

Spitz, R.A. (1959) *A Genetic Field Theory of Ego Formation*: New York, International Universities Press.

Spitz, R.A. (1965) *The First Year of Life*: New York, International Universities Press.

Stein, L. (1951) 'On talking or the communication of ideas and feelings by means of mainly audible symbols', *Brit. J. Med. Psychol.*, 24, 2.

Stein, L. (1957) 'What is a symbol supposed to be?' *J. Analyt. Psychol.*, 2, 1.

Stern, D. (1985) *The Interpersonal World of the Infant*: New York, Basic Books.

Tate, D. (1958) 'On ego development', *J. Analyt. Psychol.*, 3, 1.

Tate, D. (1961) 'Invasion and separation', *J. Analyt. Psychol.*, 6, 1.

Verney, T. and Kelly, J. (1982) *The Secret Life of the Unborn Child*: London, Sphere Books.

Wickes, F. (1966) *The Inner World of Childhood*: rev. edn: New York, Appleton-Century Crofts.

Winnicott, D.W. (1958) *Collected Papers Through Paediatrics to Psycho-Analysis*: London, Tavistock.

Winnicott, D.W. (1964) *The Child, the Family and the Outside World*: London, Penguin.

Winnicott, D.W. (1965) *The Maturational Processes and the Facilitating Environment*: London, Hogarth.

Winnicott, D.W. (1967) 'The location of cultural experience', *Int. J. Psycho-Anal.*, 48, 3.

Zimmer, H. (1951) *Philosophies of India*: London, Routledge & Kegan Paul.

Zublin, W. (1951) 'The mother figure in the fantasies of a boy suffering from early deprivation' in *Current Trends in Analytical Psychology*, ed. G. Adler: London, Tavistock.

INDEX